ARTIFICIAL INTELLIGENCE
FOR BUSINESS SUCCESS

MASTER BASIC TOOLS TO DRIVE REVENUE GROWTH,
MAXIMIZE PRODUCTIVITY & EFFICIENCY, AND
CREATE A CULTURE OF INNOVATION

B.B. JANKOSKI

CONTENTS

INTRODUCTION

If you have been wondering how other businesses are leading in the market and hitting target after target in busier times like this, it means the secret has not yet been revealed to you. However, you are in luck because I am not only going to shed light but also hand you, on a silver platter, this new, efficient extra pair of hands everyone is raving about. If, like most businesses at the forefront, you want to get ahead in your operations, creating products targeted at your customers, ensuring client satisfaction, and reaching your goals on record time, then it is time that you also deploy artificial intelligence (AI) in your operations. Most successful companies that need no introduction, like Netflix, Google, and Meta, have the added advantage of leveraging AI in their operations. In fact, recent studies reveal that over 83% of companies claim to prioritize using AI in their business strategies (Howarth, 2023). Regardless of your company size or technical expertise, if you want to emulate their success, even if your reach is only within your area or a smaller portion of the market, then considering AI technologies and tools is your best bet.

Contrary to the common belief that AI is a new kid on the block, the concept has been explored since the 1950s and has risen in popularity with more implementation from early adopters. Since its inception, AI has been explored and successfully integrated in major industries like healthcare, finance, manufacturing, customer services, and transportation. It has a reputable history of solving real-world problems like complex disease diagnosis and treatment, remote patient monitoring and personalized care plans, fraud detection and protection in financial institutions, heavy lifting of dangerous machinery in manufacturing, exploration of space and interplanetary missions, and 24-hour customer service.

The current noise around user-friendly AI tools like ChatGPT, Midjourney, and DALL-E—elaborately discussed in Chapter 3 —that are able to create human-like content by following basic prompts is the cherry on top of the capabilities of AI. This is an indication that AI has now reached the end user, working as an efficient assistant for any given task. Gone are the days when it was considered and reserved for tech giants only, because today, anyone can achieve remarkable results by tapping into the power of AI.

Given the skepticism of most people toward adopting AI, I understand your hesitation to also take the plunge into integrating this technology into your line of business. I also understand that a major part of this hesitation is usually caused by the misrepresentation of the AI concept and what it entails.

Some people believe that AI is an overhyped, passing fad that has no significant relevance to their businesses. Like most people, I used to think it was a complex theory, only reserved for technology nerds and companies with chunks of money to spend on research and trial-and-error methods. I also got exposed to the negative side of it and ruled that it is unethical and definitely something I should not associate myself with. While some of these objections are true to a certain extent, I got to learn quite late that that is not all the technology is about. The complexity and ethical issues are only scratching the surface.

There is so much more that I was leaving unexplored due to my limited knowledge and lack of involvement. Had I embraced AI earlier, I believe my business would have performed way better and sooner. That is why I am reaching out to you—to give you a lifeline no one has offered. I want you to understand that AI is more powerful than it has been given credit for. It will continue to revolutionize the business sector, and getting involved now puts you at an advantage in terms of growth and relevance with your customers. In my first book in this series, *Artificial Intelligence Pushing Boundaries: Is It Worth It?* I had a straightforward goal of depicting the concept in simple terms for anyone interested. I gave an overview of its history, benefits, and dangers while also exploring its future and trending tools. My aim now is to show you how you can successfully incorporate AI into your endeavors to widen your client reach, attract more business, and efficiently serve existing clients.

Artificial Intelligence for Business is your guide to better understanding and navigating through successful AI implementation.

It is your manual to unlocking the power of AI for your own success. Within this comprehensive book lie a plethora of opportunities and actionable steps to integrate AI into your business. I dispel myths and address ethical concerns clouding this technology while showing you ways you can responsibly embrace AI for your benefit and that of society. By the end of this book, you will be equipped with the knowledge and confidence to leverage AI for enhanced marketing and sales campaigns, improved customer service and client satisfaction, streamlined operations, increased efficiency, and data-driven decision-making for better results and business conduct. Join me as I unravel the mysteries and demonstrate successful ways of tapping into this powerful tool using easy-to-grasp natural language and less technical jargon for your better understanding.

1

INTRODUCTION TO ARTIFICIAL INTELLIGENCE

I n the intricate tapestry of technological advancement, AI emerges as a groundbreaking thread, weaving intelligence into machines and reshaping the landscape of business. This chapter serves as a gateway to the realm of AI, offering a comprehensive exploration of its definition, significance in business, and a historical journey through its evolution in the corporate sphere. AI, at its essence, embodies the simulation of human intelligence in machines, empowering them with the ability to learn, reason, and make decisions. Running a business requires humans to be able to deliver quality products or services to ensure customer satisfaction, improve efficiency, and book profits to make up for the effort and resources invested. Throughout this book, I will demonstrate how using AI systems reduces the workload, improves the speed of service delivery, and, overall, benefits the organization and its clients. In this introductory chapter, I will make you familiar with the basics of this technology and follow up with more details in succeeding chapters.

DEFINITION AND OVERVIEW OF AI

As the name hints, artificial intelligence is the ability of non-human (artificial) bodies and minds to learn, think, reason, and comprehend situations like humans do. This means having computer machines and systems that possess cognitive abilities to function and tackle tasks in a manner that humans would. At its core, AI encompasses a spectrum of capabilities, ranging from machine learning algorithms that empower systems to adapt and improve to natural language processing that enables machines to comprehend and communicate in human-like ways. This comprehension allows machines to carry out tasks that would be entrusted to humans, such as problem-solving, language understanding, pattern recognition, and decision-making. Entrusting these tasks to AI is essential in business because humans can take longer to perform them, while machines save time. Which is why companies leveraging AI continue to gain a competitive edge because they have a first-mover's advantage as AI quickly analyzes data and makes relevant decisions with favorable outcomes. It is essential to first grasp AI's multifaceted nature and overarching significance in the technological landscape.

Why Understanding AI Matters

Contrary to the way it has been depicted, AI is not a singular entity but rather a vast umbrella encompassing various technologies and techniques with applications across numerous domains. From healthcare and finance to transportation and entertainment, AI is impacting virtually every facet of our lives. You may choose to deploy it on a minimal basis, like communication, while another business might go full spectrum and model their entire operations around it. Technically, AI exists on a spectrum, from narrow AI capable of handling specific tasks with expertise (like playing chess) to general AI, the hypothetical future of machines with human-like intelligence and adaptability. The next chapter elaborates more on these types of AI because understanding these different levels is key to evaluating AI's potential and limitations.

It is also worth noting that AI is not static. It is constantly learning, evolving, and adapting thanks to advancements in algorithms, hardware, and data availability. AI is shaping the future, and understanding its capabilities and limitations helps us prepare for the changes it will bring. We are currently witnessing an AI exponential evolution, requiring us to also increase our learning speed if we do not want to remain behind. What is currently relevant and making waves as the best AI tool for a certain task can be obsolete tomorrow. Grasping this dynamic nature is vital for staying informed about the latest developments and their implications.

Moreover, AI also helps us make informed decisions. From personal choices about technology use to societal policy discussions, understanding AI empowers us to make informed decisions about its impact on our lives. Currently, most people who are skeptical about AI base their decisions on ethical considerations of this technology. You will see in Chapter 4 how AI's potential benefits are accompanied by ethical challenges such as bias, privacy, and job displacement. Understanding these challenges is crucial for the responsible development and deployment of AI technology.

THE IMPORTANCE OF AI IN BUSINESS

AI plays a pivotal role in various businesses. A great business must solve a problem, offer a service or product that customers need, and make money for you as the owner. While most businesses are still able to reach these goals without AI, those that incorporate AI into their systems achieve them on a larger scale. They are able to solve more problems, create more products and services, serve more clients, and ultimately make more money. Therefore, if you also want to widen your reach and scale your business, learning about the following AI tasks will indicate areas you can start delegating to AI.

Task Automation

There are often repetitive tasks that your employees are doing on a daily basis. For instance, capturing data, counting stock, sending recommendations, or typing emails. Most companies already entrust these monotonous tasks to virtual assistants, who process large amounts of data in seconds. You, too, can automate these routine tasks by assigning them to AI models. This frees up your staff to focus on more creative and strategic responsibilities.

Timely Decision-Making

Making tough decisions can take humans an incredible amount of time spent brainstorming and overanalyzing possible outcomes. This can cause businesses to miss out on timely deals that require fast action. AI excels at analyzing vast datasets quickly, extracting meaningful insights, and identifying patterns that may elude human analysis. Incorporating AI into your decision-making processes ensures that your business remains ahead of the competition by not missing out on any deals.

Improved Customer Experience

Imagine being able to assist your customer virtually, in real time, irrespective of your different time zones. For instance, let's assume a customer has ordered a product from your company and they realize that a wrong or faulty product has been dispatched due to human error. As soon as they realize the error, they go to your website and find a readily available AI assistant who asks them a few questions to better understand their query. The customer uploads the picture of their product, and through image recognition and natural language processing abilities, the assistant captures the claim, verifies the need to dispatch a replacement product or offer a refund, and sends the customer proof that it will be processed. At the end of the day, the customer is able to get relief from their frustration without having to wait for you or anyone in your team to manually process the claim and resolve the matter. Your team comes to an almost complete task: sign off a shipment for a replacement or process a refund, and you have a satisfied customer.

Cost Reduction

Business expenditure can take different forms, like trial-and-error methods and allocating resources to unguaranteed practices. As a human-driven business, it is natural that you may not know which process will work out best for you, so exploring a few options before deciding is normal. Working with AI models can limit resource waste and help you focus on targeted methods that optimize resources, reduce unnecessary expenses, and improve overall cost efficiency.

Fraud Detection and Risk Management

There are bad actors and chance takers in every business. With technological advances, criminals also upgrade their methods of accessing private information and resources for their own benefit. In sectors like finance, AI is crucial for fraud detection, ensuring the security and integrity of financial transactions. Deploying AI in your systems ensures that you minimize identity and resource theft or any misconduct. Moreover, AI is also able to detect potential risks and predict future trends. Knowing what to avoid enables you to manage risks and avoid costly mistakes.

Improved Accuracy and Speed

Human error exists in many aspects. A person can mistakenly capture the wrong information, send the wrong product, or miss an important detail, leading to a costly and lengthy rectification process. It is no surprise that humans go to work carrying enormous weight on their shoulders, stress from their homes, or work anxiety. All these can lead to human error, which reflects badly on any business. AI, on the other hand, has no stress or fatigue. Therefore, you can rest assured that it can process large datasets without feeling exhausted and make accurate decisions. Well, it is worth noting here that AI can still make mistakes, especially when it is still under training; however, its accuracy and processing speed often precede those of humans.

Accelerated Innovation and Growth

The rise of generative AI enables this technology to think creatively like humans do. Lately, creators and innovators are using AI for brainstorming, content creation, and idea refining. With excessive training and data processing, AI is now able to think outside the box and have a wild imagination. This helps companies reduce the time they spend on brainstorming sessions that have little success. Giving your employees access to AI can help your business be innovative and have accelerated growth.

Competitive Edge

It is possible to miss opportunities in business by focusing on things that seem to have potential on the surface but lack depth. As a business, you can bring different products to the market, not knowing which one will appeal more to your customers. While you will generate more money on the most sought-after products and services, you may lose more on market rejections and missed opportunities. AI helps companies identify and predict market trends and consumer behavior and channels them to create targeted advertising and sought-after products and services. Imagine knowing what your customer needs and being able to fulfill it before they even realize they have been seeking it. This makes you a thoughtful leader, ready to dominate the market by creating products and services that have great demand.

Enhanced Cybersecurity

One of the most important AI capabilities is detecting security breaches and responding to threats quickly. It usually takes humans longer to confirm the presence and type of malware threats. Using AI can save company resources and protect client data, preventing damage that may already be done when humans finally find the problem.

HISTORICAL BACKGROUND OF AI IN BUSINESS

A retrospective glance at the historical backdrop of AI in business reveals the roots of its integration, showcasing how it has evolved from theoretical concepts in the 1950s to becoming an indispensable tool for enterprises navigating the complexities of the modern market. The history of AI in business unfolds as an enduring narrative, a testament to innovation's capacity to shape and redefine. From its modest origins to its omnipresent role today, AI has become an indispensable ally for businesses, steering them towards enhanced efficiency, insightful decision-making, and a sustained competitive edge. As the future unfolds, AI's imprint on the business landscape will only deepen, charting a course toward a new paradigm of work, competition, and interaction.

Experimentation and Expert Systems (1950s–1980s)

The embryonic stages of AI, conceived through the visionary work of Alan Turing and his contemporaries, laid the theoretical groundwork in the mid-20th century. The Turing test entailed assessing the computer system's capability to think like a human. After the term was coined in the 1950s, AI was tested through mental games like chess. In this field, it showed its potential, as it indicated the ability of machines to produce exceptional results by excelling at specific tasks. However, practical applications were yet to manifest.

The 1960s and 1970s witnessed the dawn of expert systems—rudimentary rule-based programs attempting to replicate human expertise in specific domains. Examples of pioneering expert systems include DENDRAL, MYCIN, and XCON (eXpert CONfigurer). DENDRAL is an expert system developed in the 1960s specializing in analyzing chemical mass data. Akin to a smart chemist, DENDRAL helped identify the composition of chemical compounds, making it a valuable tool in chemistry and organic analysis. MYCIN is an expert system focused on medical diagnosis and treatment recommendations, particularly in the field of infectious diseases. As a trusted medical expert, it evaluated symptoms and recommended suitable antibiotics based on the patient's condition. In the 1970s, MYCIN sometimes outperformed human medical experts, demonstrating the groundbreaking capability of AI to work on complex tasks (Vaccalluzzo, 2023).

You would probably be more interested in XCON because it was geared more toward businesses and manufacturing. Developed in the 1970s by Carnegie Mellon University, XCON is an expert system that provides advice on configuring complex products like computer systems. Like a business advisor, XCON was a knowledgeable consultant, helping businesses customize and optimize their products based on specific requirements. It was reported that the XCON AI system saved Digital Equipment Corporation (DEC) over $40 million a year in the 1980s by processing over 80,000 orders, achieving 95%–98% accuracy, and overall increasing customer satisfaction (Chambers, 2023).

Although basic by today's standards, these systems hinted at the potential prowess of AI. The 1980s also brought a surge of interest and investment, with companies like General Electric and American Airlines pioneering AI experimentation in areas such as scheduling and forecasting. Recently, American Airlines has partnered with Google AI to work toward reducing global warming through the reduction of contrails—white lines left by planes—without increasing fuel consumption (Wilowski, 2023).

The Rise of Machine Learning, AI in Marketing, and Automation (1990s–2000s)

The 1990s ushered in a transformative era with the ascent of machine learning (ML), a game-changing technique enabling computers to learn autonomously from data. This marked a paradigm shift, empowering AI to adapt and evolve independently. Businesses seized this newfound capability, applying AI to customer segmentation, fraud detection, and supply chain optimization. Customer relationship management (CRM) systems, infused with AI, redefined customer interactions, while e-commerce giants like Amazon harnessed recommendation engines to revolutionize online shopping.

Moreover, the 1990s and 2000s also witnessed the birth of AI-driven marketing, where intelligent algorithms transformed data analysis, online advertising, and email marketing. With websites, online purchases, and email communication, the internet has generated vast amounts of customer data. AI tools like web analytics (e.g., clickstream analysis) helped marketers understand user behavior, website performance, and customer preferences. Additionally, AI algorithms analyzed customer data to identify patterns and segment audiences based on demographics, interests, and purchase history. This enabled personalized marketing campaigns, tailoring messages and recommendations for each individual, as you have seen with Amazon.

Furthermore, AI models analyzed historical data and customer behavior to predict future trends and identify potential customers. This empowered marketers to anticipate demand, optimize ad targeting, and personalize marketing efforts for maximum impact. AI algorithms also helped websites improve their ranking in search engine results pages (SERPs), ensuring greater visibility for potential customers. Tools like keyword research and backlink analysis optimize website content and strategies for organic search traffic.

Even today, AI-powered platforms like Google Ads and Bing Ads utilize algorithms to target specific audiences based on demographics, interests, and online behavior. This makes pay-per-click (PPC) advertising more efficient and cost-effective, reaching the right customers at the right time. As the internet continues to advance, AI tools also analyze social media data to understand audience sentiment, identify influencers, and optimize social media campaigns. This allows brands to engage with customers on a personal level and build strong communities around their products or services.

The Era of Big Data and AI Democratization (2010–Present)

The 2010s witnessed an explosion of digital data, propelling AI to unprecedented heights. ML algorithms have become better at handling large amounts of data and finding subtle patterns and insights within it. Cloud computing democratized AI, rendering its power accessible and affordable for businesses of all sizes. Platforms like Google Cloud and Microsoft Azure have become catalysts for AI integration. Its applications diversified across marketing, human resources, and operations, with chatbots and virtual assistants becoming integral components of the business landscape.

We are in the content creation era, and AI continues to shine. Platforms like Jasper and ShortlyAI leverage natural language processing to generate engaging content like blog posts, social media captions, and even product descriptions, freeing up marketers' time for strategic tasks. AI can also personalize video ads and audio messages based on user data and preferences, creating highly relevant and impactful experiences.

The tools that are beneficial to any business include chatbots and virtual assistants. These AI-powered conversational interfaces provide 24/7 customer support, answer questions, and offer personalized recommendations, enhancing customer satisfaction and engagement. We now have advanced algorithms that optimize website layouts and other campaign elements in real-time, maximizing conversion rates and return on investment (ROI). These algorithms also analyze customer data to identify high-potential leads, allowing sales teams to prioritize their efforts and focus on the most promising prospects.

The integration of AI in marketing and business in general is still evolving, and the future holds even more exciting possibilities. We can expect AI to personalize customer experiences to an even greater degree, predict and influence customer behavior, and automate complex marketing tasks, freeing human marketers to focus on creativity and strategic thinking. As we stand at the threshold of the 2020s, the trajectory of AI in business propels us into a future of even deeper integration. AI is poised to handle more complex tasks, automate decision-making, and personalize experiences to unprecedented degrees. AI-powered robots are poised to redefine manufacturing and logistics, blurring the lines between human and machine collaboration. The ethical dimensions of AI, including issues of bias, transparency, and job displacement, will ascend to the forefront of considerations for businesses. The next chapter takes a deeper dive into the types of AI, covering their benefits, challenges, and examples.

2

TYPES OF ARTIFICIAL INTELLIGENCE

E mbarking on the fascinating exploration of AI, this chapter delves into its diverse realms, where machines mirror and extend human intelligence. From specialized task performers in narrow AI to the hypothetical intellect of general AI and the speculative pinnacle of artificial superintelligence, each type unfolds a distinct chapter in the narrative of intelligent machines. As we navigate through these classifications, we unravel the intricacies of how AI adapts, learns, and evolves, reshaping our understanding of what machines can achieve. We will also dissect the benefits, challenges, and examples of each type for your better comprehension.

NARROW AI

Also known as "weak AI," narrow AI is the most common type of AI, focused and efficient in doing one thing and doing it incredibly well. It is meticulously crafted to excel at specific tasks, such as strategic board games or navigating complex traffic patterns. While others may consider narrow AI's ability to focus on a specific task as a weakness, that could be its very reason for being so efficient wherever it is implemented. In the realm of business and everyday life, narrow AI manifests as the driving force behind virtual assistants, recommendation algorithms, and autonomous systems. We are currently living in the era of narrow AI, although the anticipated subsequent technological advancements seem imminent.

Benefits of Narrow AI

Enhanced Efficiency and Accuracy

Narrow AI excels at specific tasks, often surpassing human capabilities in speed and precision. It has the ability to navigate complex situations in a timely fashion. As efficiency is one of every business's primary goals, narrow AI is already widely used for this benefit.

Improved Decision-Making

By analyzing vast amounts of data and identifying patterns, narrow AI can provide valuable insights and recommendations, supporting better decision-making in various fields. It leaves no stone unturned before coming up with a solution or decision.

Automation of Repetitive Tasks

As I mentioned in the previous chapter, narrow AI automates tedious and repetitive tasks, freeing up human resources for more creative and strategic endeavors. You do not want your team to be spending time doing manual jobs like data capture, product recommendations, or calculations that are no-brainers for AI tools.

24/7 Availability

Unlike humans, narrow AI systems can operate continuously, providing uninterrupted service and support. AI models do not have other responsibilities, like taking care of family and societal needs. Its job is to do what it is assigned to do without any excuse.

Customization and Personalization

Narrow AI can be tailored to specific needs and preferences, offering personalized experiences in areas like product recommendations or virtual assistants. Unlike humans, who may be biased or compare people or situations, AI treats each individual as special without making them feel secondary.

Challenges of Narrow AI

Limited scope

Narrow AI is confined to its specific domain of expertise. It lacks the broader understanding and adaptability of human intelligence. Humans can attempt any given role, even if it is not their specialty, because they are created to be multifunctional. Contrarily, although we have multimodal AI, narrow AI systems cannot do tasks beyond what they are programmed to do.

Data Dependence

The performance of narrow AI heavily relies on the quality and quantity of data it is trained on. Biases and inaccuracies in the data can lead to biased or incorrect outputs. Most narrow AI systems cannot source additional information beyond their programming. For instance, unless you update your virtual assistant with the latest company information, it can continue to give out outdated replies to clients.

Lack of Explainability

Narrow AI algorithms can be complex and opaque, making it difficult to understand why they make certain decisions or recommendations. Even if an AI system comes up with a ground-breaking solution to a problem, the fact that it cannot entirely reveal how it came up with it can raise concerns about transparency and accountability. This makes it difficult to fully entrust AI to sensitive departments where clear steps are necessary.

Job Displacement

Automation through narrow AI is already leading to job losses in certain sectors. This requires workforce retraining and adaptation for anyone who wants to remain relevant and skilled. The fear of job displacement can also negatively affect businesses, as individuals who still find this technology foreign may start underperforming due to stress or making mistakes while trying to prove their worth or secure their place in an organization.

Ethical Considerations

Biases in training data and algorithms can lead to discriminatory outcomes. Careful design and monitoring are necessary to ensure the ethical use of narrow AI. Chapter 4 elaborates on how AI in general raises ethical concerns and tackles suggested solutions.

Examples of Narrow AI

AlphaGo

Created in 2014 by the DeepMind team, AlphaGo is an AI programmed and trained by studying winners of the Go game with the intention of equipping it to win the most complex mental board game. After beating the European Go player, Fan Hui, 5-0 in its premier AI versus human match in 2015, AlphaGo also defeated the legendary 18-title world champion, Lee Sedol, in 2016. In the nerve-racking, 4-day game watched by over 200 million people, AlphaGo played the most creative and inventive winning moves, including one that had 1 in 10,000 chances of ever being used. This showcases its ability to excel at a single, highly strategic task (Google DeepMind, 2020).

Facial Recognition Technology

Facial recognition technology stands as a prominent illustration of narrow AI's capabilities, particularly in targeted visual recognition tasks. Widely employed across diverse applications, this technology has become integral to unlocking smartphones, enhancing security systems, and aiding law enforcement investigations. Narrow AI algorithms behind facial recognition systems are trained to identify and analyze unique facial features, allowing for accurate and efficient authentication processes. Despite its effectiveness in specific contexts, concerns regarding privacy, data security, and potential biases have sparked debates about the ethical implications of widespread facial recognition use. Nevertheless, the versatility and precision of facial recognition technology underscore the impactful role that narrow AI can play in specialized visual recognition applications.

Spam Filters

Spam filters are intelligent systems that efficiently identify and filter unwanted emails, highlighting narrow AI's application in everyday digital routines. These systems are designed to sift through vast volumes of incoming emails, efficiently distinguishing between legitimate messages and unwanted or potentially harmful content. The underlying technology behind spam filters involves sophisticated algorithms that analyze various attributes of an email, such as sender details, content structure, and metadata. By learning from patterns and characteristics associated with spam or phishing attempts, these narrow AI systems continually evolve to adapt to new tactics employed by malicious actors. The result is a highly effective tool that not only safeguards users from unwanted distractions but also plays a crucial role in maintaining the security and integrity of digital communication channels. The application of narrow AI in spam filters showcases the ability of artificial intelligence to enhance the user experience and cybersecurity in practical, everyday scenarios.

Self-Driving Cars

Autonomous vehicles like the Audi A8, Tesla models S, 3, X, and Y, and Mercedes EQS and S-Class models utilize narrow AI algorithms and sensory data to navigate traffic, detect obstacles, and make driving decisions, demonstrating the potential for specialized AI in transportation. While it is recommended that drivers remain alert and ready to take over in case of an emergency, this AI capability has propelled the performance of these behemoth car dealers. Mercedes witnessed an 18% increase in sales between 2022 and 2023 (Team ACV, 2023).

Medical Diagnosis Systems

Medical diagnosis systems, powered by narrow AI, play a pivotal role in healthcare by analyzing medical images and data. These systems provide valuable support to healthcare professionals, aiding in the identification of diseases and facilitating well-informed decision-making. Through the utilization of advanced algorithms, narrow AI excels at recognizing patterns and anomalies in medical images, contributing to more accurate and efficient diagnoses. From interpreting X-rays to analyzing pathology slides, these AI-driven systems enhance the speed and precision of medical assessments, ultimately improving patient outcomes. The integration of narrow AI in medical applications showcases its potential to augment the capabilities of healthcare professionals and advance the field of diagnostics.

GENERAL AI

General AI is a polymath capable of learning and adapting across diverse tasks, mirroring the breadth of human intelligence. It is the holy grail of AI—the promise of machines that can understand, learn, and reason like us. While general AI remains an aspirational goal, its realization would mark a transformative juncture where machines cease to be confined by specific applications and attain a versatile understanding akin to human intelligence. This means you can confidently trust general AI to perform tasks you would usually rely on people to carry out without fear of misconduct or malfunction.

Benefits of General AI

Universal Problem-Solving and Enhanced Human Capabilities

General AI could tackle diverse challenges that require adaptability, creativity, and complex reasoning beyond the reach of current AI. Imagine breakthroughs in scientific research, personalized education, and global problem-solving. Scientists could collaboratively work alongside AI assistants, artists could co-create with AI tools on a larger scale than they currently do, and educators could tailor learning to individual needs. General AI could augment human intelligence by providing insights, assisting with complex tasks, and collaborating on creative endeavors. Wherever there is a limitation, either with the current AI or human capacity, general AI is expected to know no bounds.

Automation of Intellectual Tasks

General AI could automate complex cognitive tasks currently performed by humans, freeing up time for higher-level thinking and creative pursuits. Imagine lawyers aided by AI in legal research, doctors supported by AI in medical diagnosis, and engineers collaborating with AI in design and development. This goes beyond simply automating monotonous tasks, as narrow AI already does. It means completely trusting AI to come up with strategic plans like humans do and considering their contribution to be of high value.

Acceleration of Knowledge Discovery

General AI could analyze vast amounts of data and identify patterns that humans might miss, leading to groundbreaking discoveries in science, technology, and medicine. Imagine AI unraveling the mysteries of the universe, developing personalized medicine, and optimizing energy production.

Challenges of General AI

Achieving True Human-Level Intelligence

Replicating the full spectrum of human intelligence, including common sense, emotions, and social awareness, remains a significant challenge. This raises concern about what will be left for humanity when there is no difference between machine and human intelligence.

Lack of Control and Explainability

Ensuring the ethical use and accountability of general AI will be critical. This will be even harder to monitor in areas where AI has been given authority and greater responsibilities, like decision-making and autonomous systems.

Societal Impact and Adaptation

The widespread integration of general AI into society will necessitate careful consideration of its impact on social structures, cultural norms, and human values. As lines continue to be blurred, this will be a serious threat to humanity and relationships, as humans may relate more to machines than to others.

Examples of General AI

LaMDA

LaMDA is a Google AI language model demonstrating a remarkable ability to hold conversations and generate human-quality text, hinting at the potential for general AI to engage in natural language processing and understanding. The integration of the current large language models (LLMs) demonstrates that general AI advancements will be even more phenomenal in the future.

DeepMind's Gato

This AI system has been trained on a diverse range of tasks, showcasing a more general ability to learn and adapt across different domains, although it still falls short of true general AI.

AI Creativity Tools

Elaborately discussed in Chapter 3, generative AI programs like ChatGPT, Midjourney, and DALL-E demonstrate the potential for future AI to generate creative content like music, art, and writing, albeit with limitations in understanding and intentionality.

Personalized Education Platforms

Imagine AI tutors that tailor educational materials and teaching methods to individual students' needs and learning styles, reflecting the potential for general AI to personalize and optimize learning experiences.

Scientific Research Assistants

General AI could further assist scientists in conducting research by analyzing vast amounts of data, formulating hypotheses, and suggesting new avenues for exploration, accelerating scientific discovery. As I mentioned earlier, the current AI narrative already does exceptional work in diagnosing diseases and helping formulate suggested patient treatments. With general AI, experts believe that medical practitioners will be able to work collaboratively to enhance healthcare and seek AI's expertise in more complex situations as it can process and analyze information faster. However, this ability threatens to replace some medical workers.

ARTIFICIAL SUPERINTELLIGENCE

Considered to be a mind beyond human comprehension, superintelligence AI surpasses not only humans but all other forms of intelligence. It is the hypothetical pinnacle, capable of solving the most intricate problems, understanding abstract concepts effortlessly, and pushing the boundaries of knowledge to unimaginable frontiers. It is a glimpse into a future where AI tackles climate change, unravels the universe's secrets, and leads humanity to unimaginable heights.

Benefits of Artificial Superintelligence

Solving Humanity's Greatest Challenges

Superintelligence could tackle global problems like climate change, poverty, and disease with unprecedented efficiency and effectiveness. Imagine AI systems optimizing energy production, developing sustainable solutions, and providing personalized healthcare to eradicate diseases regardless of current human limitations

Unlocking Unimaginable Advancements

Superintelligence could push the boundaries of human knowledge and understanding in fields like physics, mathematics, and space exploration, leading to breakthroughs beyond our current comprehension. Imagine AI unraveling the universe's mysteries, discovering new forms of energy, and colonizing other planets. The possibilities are truly unimaginable and endless.

Human Augmentation and Transcendence

Superintelligence could enhance human capabilities through brain-computer interfaces or other technologies, enabling us to access and process information beyond our current limitations. Imagine humans collaborating with AI to achieve feats of intelligence and creativity beyond what we can currently imagine.

Challenges of Artificial Superintelligence

Existential Threat

As depicted in fiction books and feature films, the potential for superintelligence to become uncontrollable or pose an existential threat to humanity is a major concern. No one knows what will happen when we have machines more intelligent than humans. It remains a scary thought. Robust safeguards and ethical frameworks will be crucial to ensuring safe and responsible development.

Human Obsolescence

If superintelligence surpasses human intelligence in all aspects, it raises questions about the role and purpose of humans in society. Besides having lazy humans incapable of making major decisions without relying on machines, human contribution might be considered unnecessary in some areas. This could lead to people feeling inadequate and irrelevant.

Loss of Control and Autonomy

If AI becomes deeply integrated into our lives and decision-making processes, it could lead to a loss of human control and autonomy, raising concerns about privacy, freedom, and democratic values. If there is no human intervention, we could be living in a world where values and morals mean nothing, and that seems like a strange world. Surely, no human wants to live a life that feels like being in a perpetual puppet show. That is possible if AI gains major control over us. This is why some experts keep warning us about being more involved and open-minded about AI so that we can learn together and be in a position to put a stop to anything that threatens humanity.

Unforeseen Consequences

The vastness and complexity of superintelligence could lead to unforeseen consequences, making it crucial to develop robust risk assessment and mitigation strategies. Although this might be considered a fear of the unknown, we cannot help but worry about the kind of future we will have.

Ethical Considerations and Philosophical Dilemmas

The development and use of superintelligence will raise profound ethical questions about the nature of consciousness, free will, and the value of human life.

Examples of Artificial Superintelligence

While still hypothetical, artificial superintelligence presents a profound and potentially transformative future. There are currently no examples, but the following theories are possible:

- Imagine an AI that could solve complex problems like climate change or world hunger, drawing upon vast knowledge and computational power beyond human capabilities.

- Think of an AI capable of understanding and explaining the universe's fundamental laws, revealing insights into the nature of reality that humans might never grasp alone.
- Consider the possibility of AI contributing to advancements in fields like medicine, technology, and energy that surpass current human comprehension, leading to unimaginable progress.

While these types of AI indicate that technological advancements will have great benefits and make our lives easier, it is important to stay alert to ensure that the technology does not advance at an uncontrollable rate. It is crucial to stay engaged and aware as the future unfolds so that we are not caught with our pants down. It is also important that we explore AI in all facets; rather than putting challenges ahead of us, we must consider using AI responsibly. The next chapter sheds more light on the popular AI tools and their role in business.

3

AI TECHNOLOGIES AND TOOLS
USED IN BUSINESS

The ever-evolving AI landscape unfolds a myriad of technologies that have become instrumental players in reshaping the business realm. Among its contributors, we see ground-breaking advancements in historic systems like ML, deep learning (DL), natural language processing (NLP), computer vision (CV), image and speech recognition, and robotics. The capabilities of these technologies continue to increase business efficiency at an interesting rate. From these AI cornerstones also emerge numerous tools beneficial for business productivity and efficiency. The trending tools are the reason you must explore AI because they demonstrate that this space is no longer limited to tech giants only but accessible to everyone.

POPULAR AI TECHNOLOGIES

There is a common misconception that AI is a singular technology operating with the same capabilities. However, it is a multi-dimensional concept that can be broken down into technological subsets depending on the levels of its various abilities. While the term AI is general, it is made up of other technologies, each specializing in different cognitive abilities. The trending individual AI tools discussed toward the end of this chapter combine one or more of the technologies described next.

Machine Learning

Machine learning is a subset of AI that enables systems to learn from data and improve performance without explicit programming. This means that the AI model is able to progressively grasp new information and use it to improve, rather than limiting its knowledge to the data that it was trained on. ML finds diverse applications, including recommendation engines, fraud detection, predictive maintenance, personalized marketing, financial forecasting, image and speech recognition for medical imaging, and voice-activated devices. It stands as a powerhouse, seamlessly automating tasks, refining decision-making, and unraveling patterns within large datasets.

These benefits make it an integral component of making any business thrive. Therefore, you can deploy ML in any area of your business where these applications are better suited, depending on your business needs. However, it is important to note that ML also comes with its own set of challenges, as is the case with any technology. Data bias, lack of explainability, model interpretability, and the need for skilled personnel are some of the major setbacks limiting this technology. This calls for human oversight at sensitive points to ensure that its applications are ethical and responsible for your business and customers.

Natural Language Processing

Natural language processing is the ability for machines to learn, understand, interpret, and generate text that humans under-stand in such a way that it is hard to tell human-generated text apart. This fosters a harmonious relationship and communica-tion between humans and machines using a universal language that both parties relate to. Therefore, major applications of NLP can be seen in chatbots, virtual assistants, sentiment analysis, machine translation, language translation, document summarization, content creation, voice search, and speech-to-text transcription. Its benefits include improving customer service, automating communication, analyzing feedback, personalizing content, facilitating global market engagement, and enhancing accessibility through voice interfaces.

Some of the shortcomings include language ambiguity, sarcasm or humor misunderstandings, and potential biases in language models. As is the case with homographs, homophones, and homonyms, sometimes words or phrases can have more than one meaning, making it tricky for machines to understand the intended message. Some of these words can have the same spelling or similar sound, making it difficult for machines to accurately understand or generate text or speech prompts. Humor and sarcasm often involve saying something but meaning the opposite. This can be challenging for machines to grasp, as they might take the words literally. For example, in a sarcastic comment like "Nice job!" after a mistake, the words praise, but the tone suggests the opposite. This makes it difficult for machines to distinguish or understand the intended meaning. Another challenge is that, if a language model is trained on biased data, it might unknowingly favor one group over another, leading to unfair or skewed results.

Computer Vision

Computer vision enables machines to interpret and make decisions based on visual data, mimicking human vision. Through the use of cameras and sensors, this technology allows systems to "see" and analyze visual data in a manner that humans would. CV is used in facial recognition, object detection, medical imaging analysis, autonomous vehicles, visual search, image-based product recommendations, and quality control. Some of its benefits include enhancing security, automating processes, and aiding in medical diagnosis. In self-driving cars, it revolutionizes transportation and personalizes user experiences through image analysis. However, you must be aware of CV's limitations, which include privacy concerns, bias in facial recognition algorithms, handling complex visual scenes, and ethical considerations in autonomous systems.

Deep Learning

As a subset of ML, deep learning also does not rely on explicit pre-programming. Instead, the system has layers of learning abilities where it continuously gets smarter the more it interacts with more data. This deep, multi-layered ability to extract information and expand its knowledge makes DL resemble the way humans learn using a multi-layered brain. The major challenge with this AI system is that sometimes humans cannot comprehend the depth of its data because it does not entirely reveal its processes. This lack of explainability can make us doubt some of its findings and question any authority it has been given. This means that, as much as it handles complex data, learns from experience, improves accuracy over time, outperforms traditional ML methods, and enhances efficiency in image and speech analysis tasks, applying it in business must be done with caution and intense supervision in sensitive areas. DL has successfully been applied in image and speech recognition, self-driving cars, natural language processing, fraud detection, anomaly detection, image and video classification, and sentiment analysis.

Robot Process Automation

Robotic process automation (RPA) involves the use of software robots to automate repetitive, rule-based tasks. While you may be familiar with robots depicted in movies carrying out instructions or operating viciously, as is the case in the *Terminator* film series, there have been advancements in the application of these non-human assistants. Initially, robots only waited to execute given instructions or solely operate based on their programming. For instance, robots that serve customers in some restaurants or those that service patients in hospitals can only do preprogrammed tasks like greeting, taking orders, delivering food or medication, handing out bills, and facilitating the payment process.

However, humanoid robots like Sophia and Ameca demonstrate an impressive upgrade, as they are able to merge all these technologies together to sort of operate independently. While these robots subtly joke and deny any possibility of robot takeover and say that they only carry out given instructions, it is alarming how they are able to handle live conversations and give appropriate responses in real-time during TV interviews. This indicates that robots can be automated or trained to function without human intervention. Another ground-breaking advancement in robots can be seen with the Rovers, which explore other planets and space adventures beyond human capability.

Using a combination of the above technologies, RPA can now automate tasks like data entry, customer service interactions, invoice processing, order fulfillment, and data extraction from images and documents. In terms of benefits, RPA improves efficiency and accuracy, reduces costs, frees human employees for higher-level tasks, and can leverage image and speech recognition for automated data capture. However, some of the challenges include limited adaptability to changing workflows, difficulty handling unstructured data, and concerns about potential job displacement.

TOP AI TOOLS FOR BUSINESS EFFICIENCY AND PRODUCTIVITY

Perhaps an in-depth explanation of the above technologies may seem complex for a business owner who just wants to understand the basic tools accessible to them. Below are a variety of AI tools that any business can incorporate into their existing models without any prior technological experience or coding skills. From content creation to designing lively websites, these tools are beginner-friendly in terms of interface and accessibility.

Content Creation and Management

ChatGPT

With core features like generating creative text formats (poems, code, and scripts), translating languages, and brainstorming ideas, ChatGPT tops the list of content creation and management tools. Arguably, ChatGPT is the reason behind the current AI frenzy and mass adoption due to its accessibility and user-friendliness. It unlocks creative potential, sparks inspiration, simplifies communication across languages, and accelerates the ideation process. While a free version works efficiently, paying a $20/month subscription unlocks a whole new world of add-on features and access to real-time data that can elevate your business to greater heights.

Google Bard

Bard uses the most sophisticated large language model (LLM) and pathways language model 2 (PaLM 2), with multilingual proficiency far surpassing the capabilities of other LLMs. This gives Bard access to a vast amount of knowledge and the ability to handle complex tasks. As a major ChatGPT rival, Bard can understand and respond to spoken language, making it a powerful tool for hands-free interaction. It can also be synchronized with other Google products, allowing seamless integration with tools like Gmail and Calendar, which enhances your workflow efficiency. Bard can generate and export code in various languages, boosting developer productivity. Moreover, it has intelligent document summarization and can extract key points and insights from complex documents quickly and effectively.

MidJourney

MidJourney is another most-loved AI tool. Its core features include creating high-quality images from text prompts, offering artistic styles and variations, and allowing detailed control. It enhances visual communication, inspires product design, generates engaging social media content, and saves time on image creation. Accessing MidJourney simply requires you to join its Discord channel for free and start creating. The free access allows you to see what other creators (including your competition) are doing and also publishes your creations on a channel accessible to everyone. If you want to keep your content private, you can upgrade to a premium account.

DALL-E 3

DALL-E 3 generates photorealistic and surreal images, offers multiple editing features, and excels at concept art and detailed compositions. It can also comprehend complex language like idioms and expressions, create cinematic concepts, and conceptualize creative ideas. As a result, DALL-E 3 creates impactful visuals for advertising, marketing, and branding, pushes the boundaries of visual storytelling, and expands creative options.

Jasper

Jasper is an AI writing assistant for generating various content formats, such as blog posts, social media captions, and product descriptions. Its core features include tailoring style to brand voice, retrieving real-time information, and integrating with workflows. Integrating Jasper into your business means that you will boost content output, enhance brand consistency, simplify research, and streamline the content creation process.

ShortlyAI

Also great for a writing business, ShortlyAI offers long-form content creation, plagiarism checking, research assistance, and topic suggestions. It saves time writing complex content, ensures originality, provides research support, and expands creative brainstorming.

Grammarly

Similar to ShortlyAI, Grammarly also has the following core features: grammar and style correction, clarity improvement, vocabulary suggestions, and plagiarism detection. It elevates writing quality, enhances professionalism, minimizes errors, and increases confidence in communication.

Copysmith

Gone are the days when you had to pay lots of money to acquire a professional copywriter. With core features like generating engaging ad copy, landing pages, and marketing emails, Copysmith analyzes competitors' content and suggests keywords that will enhance your content. It also creates high-converting marketing materials, simplifies campaign development, and gains insights from market competition.

Project and Time Management

Asana

Asana is a great AI tool for task automation, progress tracking, team collaboration, file sharing, and communication. It streamlines workflows, improves team accountability, enhances project visibility, and centralizes team communication. Your team can greatly benefit from using this AI-powered project management tool.

Monday.com

Similar to Asana, Monday.com has incredible core features, like customizable workflows, automation capabilities, visual dashboards, and integrations with various tools. It provides flexibility in project management, automates repetitive tasks, offers real-time project insights, and fosters collaboration across teams.

Notion

Notion features an all-in-one workspace for notes, tasks, projects, wikis, and databases, as well as AI-powered search and organization. Moreover, it consolidates information in one place, improves knowledge management, simplifies task organization, and empowers cross-functional collaboration.

Todoist

Todoist is another popular project management software with core features like smart scheduling, recurring tasks, priority sorting, labels and filters, and progress tracking. This tool optimizes task scheduling, simplifies task prioritization, enhances personal productivity, and ensures efficient day-to-day operations.

Duet

Although not yet publicly available, Duet is the brainchild of Google AI and will revolutionize this space. Duet's main focus is integrating AI into Google Workspace tools to enhance productivity and collaboration. For example, suggesting relevant documents, summarizing emails, and generating draft text. Its target audience is Google Workspace users, primarily businesses and organizations. Currently, only select users are testing Duet.

Customer Service and Engagement

ChatSpot.ai by HubSpot

ChatSpot.ai enhances productivity through a conversational customer relationship management (CRM) bot. It also enables users to gather necessary CRM data directly within the chat interface. Moreover, it provides templates for prospecting, streamlining outreach efforts. ChatSpot.ai also generates images from text inputs using AI, adding visual elements to communication. It can also help facilitate in-depth exploration of company data, aiding in informed decision-making.

Drift

With advanced core features like live chat functionality, lead generation tools, conversational marketing automation, and customer data tracking, Drift provides instant customer support, streamlines lead capture, personalizes customer interactions, and improves conversion rates.

Amelia

With core features like answering customer questions, resolving issues, providing self-service options, and integrating with CRM systems, Amelia scales customer support capabilities, reduces reliance on human agents, provides 24/7 customer service, and improves issue resolution time.

Intercom

Intercom has personalized messaging, automated support workflows, customer feedback analysis, and sentiment monitoring. Its benefits include delivering proactive customer service, automating repetitive tasks, gathering valuable customer insights, and improving customer satisfaction.

Data Analysis and Reporting

ThoughtSpot Sage

Sage is integrated with core features like natural language search for data exploration, AI-generated insights, data visualization tools, and collaboration features. It makes data accessible to everyone, simplifies complex data analysis, uncovers hidden trends and patterns, and drives data-driven decision-making. As you type, Sage intelligently suggests relevant questions and keywords to refine your search. With its human-in-the-loop feedback system, users can provide feedback on Sage's suggestions and results, improving its accuracy over time. It can automate some data modeling tasks, saving data analysts time and effort.

Productivity

TheGist

With core features like AI-powered text summarization and extracting key points from documents, articles, and emails, theGist benefits businesses by improving information comprehension. It also speeds up research, simplifies communication, and generates concise reports and meeting notes. With its ability to be integrated into multiple tools like Slack, WhatsApp, GitHub, and HubSpot with a smooth switch from each app, theGist is ideal for teams dealing with information overload.

Lavender.ai

Lavender.ai generates different creative text formats like poems, scripts, musical pieces, and marketing copy based on user input. It is an efficient tool that can be helpful for brainstorming and overcoming writer's block. In business, Lavender.ai boosts marketing creativity, inspires content creation, personalizes customer interactions, and adds a unique touch to branding.

Frase.ai

Frase.ai is essential for any business with an online presence. With core features like optimizing content for search engines (SEO) by analyzing keywords, competitors, and user intent, it improves website traffic, leads, and conversions, optimizes content creation efforts, and gains insights into audience preferences.

Fireflies.ai

With the ability to automate data extraction from complex documents, tables, and PDFs., Fireflies saves businesses time and resources spent on data entry, improves data accuracy, streamlines workflows, and allows for faster analysis and decision-making. It is useful for any business dealing with large amounts of data.

Web Creation

Hostinger AI Website Builder

Hostinger is a perfect AI tool for businesses requiring web creation and e-commerce features without using any complex code. Anyone with no prior coding or website-building skills can simply drag and drop elements and objects into a template and edit them to fit their brand preferences. Hostinger is always learning and improving based on user interactions, keeping up with the latest design trends.

Wix Studio

Wix Studio is also another popular web creation platform leveraging AI to simplify things for anyone with no prior skills. It allows affordable hosting and is already connected to a marketplace that can help any e-commerce business.

10Web

With its built-in question-and-answer feature, 10Web is an AI website-building tool that helps businesses create websites in minutes by simply answering a few questions about their business. It can also help bring to life any WordPress website with great AI-created images.

AppyPie

Perfect for any business requiring a website or a mobile application, AppyPie provides a range of creative design tools. With its text-image generator, photo enhancer, and animation features, AppyPie makes web creation a breeze. Small businesses can also take advantage of the free four monthly projects and upgrade as needed.

TIPS FOR CHOOSING AND INCORPORATING EFFECTIVE AI TECHNOLOGIES INTO YOUR BUSINESS

Choosing the top AI tools for business productivity and efficiency can be overwhelming, as the landscape is constantly evolving and diverse. Remember, the goal is to enhance your operations strategically and empower your team with tools that align seamlessly with your business objectives. The best options for your business will depend on your specific needs, budget, and team size. The following tips can help you make a better choice of tools that will have a significant impact on your business.

Thoroughly Identify Pain Points and Areas for Improvement

Before delving into AI solutions, conduct a comprehensive analysis of your business operations. Identify the specific pain points and areas where improvements are needed. Whether it is streamlining processes, enhancing customer experiences, or optimizing decision-making, a clear understanding of your challenges is fundamental to choosing the right AI tools.

Emphasize Specific Needs Over Broad Capabilities

While the allure of all-encompassing AI tools is enticing, it is often more effective to focus on solutions that address your business's specific needs. Therefore, you must tailor your selection to tools that directly target your identified pain points, ensuring a more precise and impactful integration into your existing workflows. This will save you money and time spent on training your staff on tools that bring non-effective change to your business.

Consider Ease of Use and Integration

A user-friendly interface and seamless integration with your current systems are paramount. It is important to opt for AI tools that align with your team's skill set and can be incorporated into your workflow without causing disruptions. This ensures a smoother adoption process and maximizes the tool's effectiveness within your business environment.

Start Small and Scale Up

Rather than implementing AI tools across the entire organization at once, initiate small-scale pilot projects. This approach allows you to assess the tool's performance in a controlled environment, identify potential challenges, and fine-tune its integration. Once the pilot proves successful, you can confidently scale up, minimizing risks and optimizing the tool's impact.

Seek Expert Assistance and Utilize Free Trials

It is no secret that AI can be complex, and seeking guidance from experts in the field can provide valuable insights. Additionally, take advantage of the free trials offered by many

AI tool providers. This hands-on experience allows you to evaluate the tool's functionality, gauge its compatibility with your business needs, and make informed decisions without committing resources upfront.

From understanding major AI technologies and how they transform various industries to implementing individual AI tools, there is a level of entry for anyone wanting to leverage AI. This chapter also clarified how you can smoothly transition from traditionally running your business to exploring different ways to incorporate AI into your systems. Considering your team size, experience, and budget, starting small and scaling up is one of the incredible tips to leverage AI in an orderly manner. The next chapter delves into a controversial topic about AI ethical considerations.

4

ETHICAL CONSIDERATIONS IN AI

The ethical landscape of AI in business is complex and multifaceted, demanding careful attention to ensure responsible and equitable implementation. When it comes to AI ethics, businesses are at a vantage point to reach a wider audience and teach the masses about the responsible use of AI. Organizations consist of stakeholders, employees, and customers, all of whom need to be aware of a business's AI integration. Arguably, many individuals who are hesitant to embrace AI are driven by ethical reservations about its potential impact. There is a debate around issues around data privacy, bias, transparency, and job displacement resulting from AI implementations. This chapter brings home the subject of ethical practices associated with AI, covering the good and the bad so that business leaders like you choose to do better.

THE ETHICAL IMPLICATIONS OF AI IN BUSINESS

The impact of AI can be seen across different industries where this technology is implemented. The issue of ethics is at the top of the list of major concerns regarding this fast-growing innovation. While there are general ethical conundrums affecting the AI space, we will focus more on how they apply in business so that leaders are aware of these issues and inspired to take positive action.

Bias

Businesses can implement AI in various areas to ease their teams and improve efficiency. However, one pressing concern is the potential for bias in AI systems, which can perpetuate existing biases in data and lead to discriminatory outcomes in areas like hiring, lending, customer service, and criminal justice, leading to unfair treatment of individuals and groups. Imagine a hiring algorithm trained on resumes from the past decade. If that data disproportionately favored male applicants, the algorithm might unknowingly replicate that bias, leading to unfair hiring practices against women. Businesses deploying biased AI can face serious reputational damage if their practices come to light, leading to lost customers and investor trust.

Transparency

Some business leaders can go as far as researching, testing, and later implementing AI pilot projects without fully disclosing their intentions to the rest of their team. While they often see no harm in trying out the technology without alarming everyone, this remains unethical on so many levels. Even if they are not fired, people feel betrayed when they find out that there is a slight possibility that their jobs might be in danger.

Job Displacement

There is a rising concern that using highly autonomous AI tools will lead to job displacement. I would like to believe that your aim is not to contribute to the high unemployment rate by replacing human beings with financial responsibilities with machines. Some business leaders may be obsessed with the financial benefits of using AI and, in turn, ignore how this hurts their human resources. As you deploy AI tools to handle certain tasks to improve efficiency and minimize costs, it is important to consider how you can achieve this without leaving your employees out of jobs.

Data Privacy

Privacy is another paramount ethical consideration, particularly when it comes to collecting and analyzing sensitive personal data. AI technology has the potential to gather and analyze vast amounts of personal information, which inevitably triggers worries about individual privacy and data protection. How does your business obtain and use customer data? Using AI tools that monitor customer behavior and predict their sentiments regarding product engagement may be frowned upon by many.

Safety

Once deployed, autonomous systems operate independently, raising concerns about accountability and potentially irreversible consequences. Imagine rogue algorithms making life-or-death decisions with no human oversight. Determining responsibility for casualties caused by AI poses significant ethical and legal questions. Who is accountable: the programmer, the commander, or the AI itself? Moreover, as the technological landscape takes shape in a positive way, there are people intending to use it negatively. Bad actors can misuse AI to create harmful, autonomous weapons that threaten human safety. The main concern is that AI advancements are happening at a faster rate than government regulations and law enforcement departments with technological understanding.

Explainability

Advanced AI technologies, like DL, are known to contribute to the lack of explainability of AI. Because AI systems are designed to think independently and not rely only on the data they are trained on, it is possible that sometimes they obtain favorable results from complex problems without disclosing their methods. Lack of explainability leads to questionable data. Imagine an AI model used to diagnose a rare disease. Even though doctors agree that the model's diagnosis is most likely correct, it leaves unanswered questions when it does not fully reveal how it got that diagnosis. Using this data requires responsible, transparent, and accountable business leaders who will not shift the blame to this technology at any critical stage.

ENSURING TRANSPARENCY, FAIRNESS, AND ACCOUNTABILITY IN AI-DRIVEN DECISION-MAKING

Transparency, fairness, and accountability are integral components of an ethical framework for AI in business. Businesses must be open, inclusive, and responsible in how they plan to deploy AI in their decision-making. By adopting these principles, businesses can not only navigate the ethical challenges associated with AI but also contribute to the development of responsible and trustworthy AI systems.

Being transparent about the use of AI is a fundamental ethical principle that businesses should uphold. Transparency involves openly communicating how AI is integrated into various aspects of operations. This includes providing information about the types of AI systems employed, the specific data collected and utilized, and the nature of decisions made by these AI systems. If your business decides to use AI in recruiting and hiring, candidates and employees deserve to know how AI collects, processes, and uses their data to make hiring decisions. Similarly, if AI also monitors customer behavior to improve its predictive analysis and personalize products and marketing based on customers' preferences, you must clearly communicate it. Clear communication helps build trust with stakeholders, such as customers, employees, and the wider community, fostering understanding and awareness regarding the role of AI in business processes.

Designing AI systems to be fair and unbiased is a crucial step to mitigate the risk of discriminatory outcomes. Businesses should prioritize fairness by implementing measures that prevent bias in AI algorithms. There have been cases where AI-based decisions perpetuated existing biases. For instance, prioritizing men or white people for executive, high-paying jobs and leaving low-income positions to women, black people, and people of color Regular testing for bias is essential, involving comprehensive assessments of how AI systems treat different racial or gender groups and ensuring that the algorithms do not inadvertently favor or disadvantage specific demographics. Unbiased AI systems can benefit both individuals and businesses. By proactively addressing bias, businesses can contribute to more equitable AI applications Moreover, diverse and inclusive AI systems can also lead to more creative and innovative solutions, fostering a more competitive advantage.

Holding AI systems accountable for their decisions is an ethical imperative. Establishing processes to review and challenge AI-driven decisions ensures that there is oversight and accountability for the outcomes generated by AI. This involves creating mechanisms for humans to intervene when necessary, especially in cases where the AI system's decision-making might have significant consequences. Accountability mechanisms contribute to responsible AI governance and help address concerns related to transparency, fairness, and ethical use.

GUIDELINES FOR ETHICAL AND RESPONSIBLE USE OF AI IN BUSINESS

It is crucial for businesses to establish clear ethical guidelines for the development and deployment of AI systems within their organizations. By demonstrating a commitment to ethical AI, businesses can build trust with customers, employees, and stakeholders.

Be Strategic

Before diving headfirst into AI adoption, it is crucial to develop a comprehensive vision for how AI can align with your organization's overall mission. This involves ensuring that your employees comprehend the role AI will play in your broader strategy and how it will support your organization's goals. A key aspect of this vision should be a well-defined governance framework that outlines how AI will be used in a transparent, ethical, and responsible manner. This framework should also include guidelines for employees on how they can and cannot use AI in their work. By establishing a clear vision and governance structure, you can ensure that your organization's AI adoption is strategic, responsible, and effective.

Accountability

There needs to be a clearly defined line indicating that human beings are responsible AI users. Even if AI models are assigned more authoritative roles, people must always be ready to take responsibility for the emergence of any fallout. AI systems are created to be helpers, meaning they have no full control over their assigned tasks. Responsible AI use entails keeping humans accountable at all times.

Bias Detection and Mitigation

Identifying and addressing biases embedded in training data and algorithms is crucial, as it ensures that AI decisions are fair and unbiased. This can involve human-in-the-loop approaches where human oversight ensures fairness in AI decisions. This means someone in the organization must ensure that there is no skewed data that puts others at a disadvantage.

Data Diversification

Data diversification is a crucial step towards creating robust, fair, and representative ML models. By exposing AI models to a wide range of datasets that encapsulate the diversity of real-world scenarios, we can ensure that they are better equipped to handle various situations and are not biased toward any particular group or demographic. For instance, consider facial recognition technology. If the training data is predominantly made up of individuals from a single ethnic group, the model may struggle to accurately identify faces from other groups. By diversifying the training data to include faces from a broader range of ethnicities, the model can learn to recognize and classify faces more accurately and inclusively. In essence, data diversification is essential to mitigate biases and improve the accuracy of AI models. By incorporating a broad spectrum of examples, we can create AI systems that are more inclusive and effective in handling a variety of situations.

Data Anonymization

Businesses often anonymize data to comply with regulations or protect individual privacy. This allows for valuable data analysis and research while seemingly masking personal information. Data anonymization, while seemingly a straightforward privacy solution, is not always foolproof. Therefore, it is crucial for businesses to acknowledge the complexities and potential pitfalls of anonymization to truly ensure data privacy. Explore generating synthetic data sets that retain statistical relevance but lack identifiable individuals. This allows for similar data analysis without compromising privacy. Implement robust security measures to protect the anonymized data itself. Furthermore, strong encryption, access controls, and audit trails can minimize the risk of unauthorized access or use. Businesses must be transparent about their data anonymization practices and accountable for their effectiveness. Inform individuals whose data is being used and provide mechanisms for them to control its use.

Encourage Upskilling

Encourage your team to learn more about this evolving technology and upgrade their skills. While AI is replacing some jobs, there are numerous others that will arise around this technology. No one needs to be left behind. Instead of letting your unskilled employees go, it is more ethical to provide training to your teams so that they grow with your organization. This way, you preserve jobs while implementing the technology within your organization. Doing this also ensures you have a team ready to explore and collaborate with future AI advancements.

Public Awareness and Education

Business leaders are at an advantage in advocating for public awareness regarding the rise of AI and investing in educating the masses so that people know how it impacts their lives. There must be more open-source AI systems so that people who cannot afford premium ones can still learn from and benefit from this digital space.

Use Disclaimers

As a business leveraging AI, it is crucial to inform everyone affected that you are exploring or considering integrating AI into your systems. Customers need to be aware of how their data will be used in the further training of AI models. They must also give their consent where possible. Similarly, employees must also be given a chance to process how AI implementation will affect their current and future roles in an organization.

Prioritize Employees Well-Being

To ensure the continued well-being of individuals, it is crucial to prioritize health and wellness in the workplace and other areas where AI tools and programs are being utilized. Regular check-ins and monitoring are necessary to prevent any adverse effects on mental and physical health due to prolonged exposure to these technologies. While some employees may initially feel overwhelmed as they adjust to the new systems, it is imperative to prioritize their health and well-being above all else. By doing so, we can ensure a safe and productive work environment for everyone.

Freedom to Participate

Regardless of the size of an organization, it is crucial that employees and customers are given the freedom to decide whether or not they want to participate in AI-powered programs. Everyone deserves the right to make an informed choice, even if it is just on a trial basis. And if they change their mind later on, they should be able to easily and freely withdraw without having to provide any explanations. The bottom line is that no one should be coerced or pressured into participating in these programs against their will.

Follow Official Procedures

It is important to have clear guidelines and methods in place to prevent biases in AI systems. Regulatory organizations like the European Union (EU), Federal Trade Commission (FTC), and Equal Employee Opportunity Commission (EEOC) are actively working to ensure that AI developers and companies use the technology responsibly and ethically. These organizations are ensuring that AI systems are fair and unbiased and that they are used for the benefit of society as a whole. It is important to note that the regulatory landscape is constantly evolving as AI technology progresses, and ethical considerations remain an ongoing discussion. However, by actively implementing ethical frameworks, auditing techniques, dedicated tools, and embracing regulatory oversight, businesses can ensure that AI serves the good of society and helps create a fairer and more just world.

Consider Collaboration Over Full Autonomy

While some mundane tasks can be fully entrusted to AI models to free the staff for more creative roles, this autonomy requires careful consideration. It is paramount that business leaders focus on assistive AI deployment that complements the abilities of the staff. While some people criticized the limitations of self-driving cars upon hearing that the driver or passenger must be alert and ready to take control of the car in case of an emergency, this is a great way of collaborating with AI. It is the car manufacturers who need to be transparent when advertising these autonomous cars. They should fully disclose that the cars still require conscious passengers and not oversell the dream that the car can fully control itself. Even if it is at the bare minimum, humans still need to be responsible.

Innovative companies must include their teams when implementing AI so that they get firsthand experience of how AI models work and also learn from machines. This way, there will be collaboration between humans and machines instead of either party replacing the other.

The topic of AI ethical considerations will remain ongoing because this technological landscape is not static. What is acceptable today may be an issue in the future, and vice versa. It is paramount that businesses remain engaged so that they are aware of any new regulations in order to stay on the good side of the law and morals. The next chapter will discuss the process of implementing AI in businesses.

5

IMPLEMENTING ARTIFICIAL INTELLIGENCE IN BUSINESS PROCESSES

I n today's fast-paced and highly competitive business environment, companies are under constant pressure to optimize, innovate, and stay ahead of the curve. Studies show that a significant majority of Fortune 500 companies, along with countless businesses across various sectors, are actively leveraging AI. As you have seen with the top trending AI tools in Chapter 3, AI is now a tangible tool that has the potential to revolutionize the way businesses operate. This chapter will delve into the practical aspects of implementing AI across various business processes, exploring the challenges and opportunities that lie ahead. It also covers real-world, relatable examples of behemoth companies ahead of this innovative technology.

STEPS FOR SUCCESSFULLY INTEGRATING AI INTO EXISTING BUSINESS PROCESSES

Contrary to the common belief that implementing AI in business is expensive, there are friendly ways to gradually introduce this technology without heavily investing in knowledge and resources. You do not have to change your entire business model or create a new system. Below are the useful steps you can take at your own pace to start your AI journey.

Get Familiar With AI

As the leader of your organization, it is important that you fully understand what AI entails and its capabilities. If you must attend seminars, read books, or take courses on the subject, ensure that you gather as much information as possible. Even if you will still get an expert to train your team and help you successfully onboard everyone, you must have basic knowledge of the processes involved. This will ensure that, at any point, you are aware of ethical considerations, responsible AI usage, potential risks, and areas that require attention. You will also identify the areas where your organization must prioritize AI and the possible outcomes before you even bring it to the team. You will identify problems that AI can solve and explore your company's needs so that you can focus on them. Reading this book and similar ones on the topic is a step in the right direction. My first book in this series, *Artificial Intelligence Pushing Boundaries: Is It Worth It?*, offers the most simplified version of this technology. I highly recommend it for anyone wanting to get familiar with AI without cracking their skull.

Identify Opportunities for AI Implementation

To identify areas where implementing AI will be impactful, it is important to conduct a process audit. Therefore, you must analyze your current workflows to identify repetitive tasks that can be automated, areas prone to human error, and decisions relying on intuition or incomplete data. Additionally, you must consider industry trends to be up-to-date with areas where AI shines. Research how other businesses in your sector are leveraging AI and identify potential applications relevant to your specific challenges and goals. Furthermore, evaluate the potential ROI and impact of AI on each identified opportunity. Focus on areas with high potential for efficiency gains, cost reduction, or improved decision-making.

Assess the Potential Risks and Benefits of AI

Before adopting any trendy AI tools, you must do your own due diligence to identify potential risks. While some technologies and tools may have a great reputation, you must consider their ethical implications, data privacy concerns, potential job displacement, and the need for ongoing maintenance and updates. These general AI risks do not only affect society on a large scale but will be felt more at the grassroots level. Therefore, you must consider how they will play out in your organization. Perhaps you will be more vigilant and ensure that there will be no ethics violated based on how you plan to integrate AI into your systems.

Once you have evaluated the possible risks, weigh them against the potential benefits and what your business stands to gain through AI. Analyze the potential for improved accuracy, efficiency, customer satisfaction, and competitive advantage. Maybe implementing AI will reduce costly mistakes and improve the functionality of your business. You may also find out that using AI helps you service your clients better, even if you have not seen the financial reward yet. Or perhaps you are able to rise above your competitors and gain trendsetter status, whatever is important to you. Conduct a cost-benefit analysis by comparing the expected benefits of AI integration with the implementation and maintenance costs to ensure a positive ROI. If you are comfortable with the opportunity cost, then you will not frown upon your decision to forgo the benefits.

Develop a Plan for AI Adoption

If, indeed, you decide to go through with integrating AI into your system, you will need to come up with an executable plan that will fit right into your existing business model with minimal to no disruption. Be sure to define clear goals and objectives. This means setting specific, measurable, achievable, relevant, and time-bound (SMART) goals for your AI initiative. As highlighted in Chapter 3, choose the right AI tools and technologies that align with your business and future goals. Research and select the AI solutions that best suit your identified opportunities, budget, and technical expertise.

Another integral step toward smooth AI adoption is preparing your team for change. No one wants to be caught off-guard.

Change is usually disruptive; however, you can minimize that by training your employees on the new technology and addressing any concerns or anxieties about AI integration. Part of good AI ethical practices is ensuring that no one is forced to embrace what they are not comfortable with. You may have key players in your team who are skeptical about AI, just as you were before you developed understanding. It is your job to ensure that people are well-trained and given an opportunity to decide their level of involvement.

Once your team is onboard, you must develop a data strategy. Ensure you have access to high-quality, relevant data to train and maintain your AI models. You want AI models that fit like a glove into your existing systems, and that entails extensively training them in everything important to your organization. Remember that AI will take over some responsibilities where you grant it access; therefore, there must not be any signs of inefficiency due to inadequate training.

Implement the AI Strategy

For a smooth implementation, do not overwhelm your team or systems. Rather, start small and scale gradually. Begin with pilot projects in specific areas to test the effectiveness of your AI solution before implementing it across the entire organization. Ensure seamless integration of your AI solution with your existing workflows and software to avoid disruption and data silos. If it means adopting AI only for your customer relations for the first 6–12 months, stick to this plan before overwhelming your team so that you can monitor the effectiveness of the integrated tools. Then, if you are happy with the progress, you can adjust and expand accordingly until you have a new system operating seamlessly like a well-oiled machine.

Monitor and Evaluate the AI Solution

You must continuously monitor the performance of your AI solution and adjust your approach based on the results. Keep track of the key performance indicators specific to your industry and overall goals. It could be tracking your profit margins, customer satisfaction, or order fulfillment time. Define those specific metrics to measure the impact of your AI solution on your business goals and objectives. One way to gather feedback is by asking employees, customers, and other relevant stakeholders for input. This will help you identify areas for improvement and ensure alignment with their needs. Do not just stop at getting feedback and doing nothing with it. You must continuously evaluate and improve your AI solution based on the gathered data and feedback. Remember, successful AI integration is an ongoing process. Be prepared to learn, adapt, and adjust your approach as you gain experience and the technology evolves.

CHALLENGES AND BEST PRACTICES IN AI IMPLEMENTATION

As you have already seen, implementing AI in any business comes with colossal advantages. Improving your business efficiency and witnessing your profit margins skyrocket are enough reasons to model pioneers already benefiting from this technology. However, it is worth considering that nothing will be a smooth sail; otherwise, all businesses would have long joined the AI craze. There are challenges that come with changing the way your business has always operated and introducing a new structure and way of conducting business. This section covers several roadblocks that prevent AI implementation from becoming smooth sailing. Additionally, it offers a solution to some of the challenges to make it, at least, doable and less restrictive.

Challenges

Cost

Building and implementing AI solutions can require significant investments in hardware, software, data preparation, and expertise. Unless you consider the financial requirements of AI development and deployment and how they will impact your budget, implementing AI might be a farfetched idea for you. While most AI tools come free of charge, accessing premium quality, ensuring your data privacy, and customizing them to fit your existing business model requires financial commitment. Even if you have the initial budget to integrate AI into your systems, it is important to understand that there will be ongoing maintenance and updates required. Maintaining and updating AI models to ensure accuracy and effectiveness over time incurs additional costs. Therefore, you must factor in the potential costs of adopting AI.

Complexity

Another major stumbling block, for skeptics and enthusiasts alike, is the perceived complexity surrounding AI. Besides the common belief that one must be a computer or math nerd to understand the nitty-gritty of this technology, it is also no secret that implementing and managing AI systems can require technical expertise. Understanding how AI models make decisions and explaining their reasoning can be complex, leading to concerns about transparency and accountability. There will be a need for specialized skills and knowledge to operate the new system and still maintain great performance and client satisfaction. While you can have your staff trained, it is important to remember that people have different comprehension levels. Therefore, you must be prepared because this could potentially create a talent gap within your organization.

Data Requirements

Training effective AI models requires access to large amounts of high-quality, relevant data, which may be unavailable or expensive to acquire. If you want to maintain your brand voice while rising above competition, you must be aware that you will need to invest in training AI models with vast amounts of data about your organization and industry to teach them to mimic and surpass your staff in competence. Additionally, collecting and processing personal data for AI training raises ethical concerns around privacy and data security. AI models can perpetuate biases present in the data they are trained on, leading to unfair or discriminatory outcomes. Therefore, it is your job to ensure that you eliminate existing bias and unfairness from the data the models rely on. You will need to address the ethical challenges you might face when implementing AI and ensure the responsible use of data.

Best Practices

Start Small and Scale Later

Begin with small pilot projects in specific areas with high potential for improvement and gather valuable insights before scaling up. To eliminate the complexity and initial costs, break down your AI initiatives into smaller, manageable modules. Validate the feasibility and potential impact of your AI solution before making a significant investment. This will reduce the initial financial burden and facilitate incremental scaling. You will also get to see the impact of implementing AI beforehand and adjust if there are no complications. Pilot projects allow you to gradually and smoothly integrate AI without overwhelming your team and exhausting your resources. Therefore, you must implement AI in phases, allowing for continuous learning, adaptation, and improvement based on real-world data and feedback.

Secure Buy-In and Collaboration

Involve key stakeholders (employees, customers, and regulators) in the planning and implementation process to address concerns and ensure alignment with overall business goals. Many people are already threatened by the "AI takeover." Ease the fears of your team by building trust and communication instead of being sneaky and trying out the technology in secret and surprising them later. Foster transparency and open communication about AI's role in the organization to address potential anxieties.

Prioritize Data and Ethics

As you have covered in the previous chapter, it is paramount that you implement robust data governance practices to ensure data quality, security, and compliance with ethical guidelines. Actively identify and mitigate potential biases in your data and AI models to ensure fairness and inclusivity.

Invest in Talent and Education

Because automation through AI has the potential to displace workers in certain roles, you must aim to equip your workforce with the necessary skills and knowledge to understand and work with AI effectively. This requires careful planning and re-skilling initiatives. Build a competitive strategy to attract and retain AI expertise within your organization.

REAL-WORLD EXAMPLES OF SUCCESSFUL AI IMPLEMENTATIONS IN BUSINESS

Successfully implementing AI in any business takes an organization's commitment, from finances to expertise and human resources. The giant companies below are not only paving the way for AI integration but also fully taking advantage of this disruptive technology. I chose these well-known companies as examples because they already show diversification. This demonstrates that AI has no limitations when it comes to different industries, which is a great way to inspire any business that wants to leverage AI.

Amazon

Amazon employs AI algorithms to analyze user behavior, preferences, and purchase history. This enables the platform to provide personalized product recommendations, enhance the user experience, and drive sales. AI plays a crucial role in optimizing Amazon's vast supply chain. Predictive analytics and ML algorithms help forecast demand, manage inventory efficiently, and streamline logistics, ensuring timely deliveries and minimizing costs. Furthermore, Amazon leverages AI for innovative product and service development. From voice-activated devices like Alexa to AI-powered cloud computing services, Amazon continues to explore new frontiers in technology.

Netflix

Netflix relies heavily on AI-driven recommendation algorithms to analyze user viewing patterns, preferences, and ratings. These algorithms suggest personalized movie and TV show recommendations, enhancing user engagement and retention. AI enables Netflix to personalize the presentation of its content, tailoring the user interface based on individual preferences. This ensures that users have a more customized and enjoyable viewing experience.

Google

Google's search engine is powered by AI algorithms that continuously learn and adapt to user behavior. These algorithms enhance search accuracy, providing more relevant and personalized results based on user queries. Additionally, Google Translate utilizes ML for language translation. The system learns from a vast dataset of multilingual content to provide accurate and contextually relevant translations across multiple languages. Google also invests heavily in AI research and development, leading to the creation of new products and services. Projects like Google Brain, DeepMind, and various AI-powered applications demonstrate the company's commitment to pushing the boundaries of technology.

Tesla

Tesla's pioneering spirit under Elon Musk's leadership has propelled them to the forefront of AI-powered self-driving car technology, redefining the future of transportation. Tesla vehicles are equipped with a symphony of sensors, including cameras, radar, lidar, and ultrasonic sensors. These constantly gather data on the surrounding environment, creating a detailed real-time picture of the road, obstacles, and other vehicles. Powerful AI algorithms, trained on massive datasets of driving situations, take the baton and process this sensor data. They identify objects, predict their movements, and even anticipate potential hazards like sudden lane changes or unseen pedestrians.

Furthermore, advanced algorithms map the surrounding environment in real-time, creating a dynamic and accurate representation of the road ahead. This map includes not only lane markings and traffic signals but also the positions and trajectories of other vehicles, pedestrians, and even cyclists. Using the processed data and the generated map, the AI makes split-second decisions about steering, acceleration, and braking. It navigates complex traffic scenarios, maintains safe distances, and even adapts to unpredictable situations like sudden weather changes or road closures.

AI is not just about safety; it can also enhance the driving experience. Features like adaptive cruise control and lane-keeping assistance rely on AI to provide a smooth and effortless driving experience, reducing fatigue and stress. Tesla's AI systems are constantly learning and evolving. Every mile driven by its fleet of vehicles generates valuable data that is fed back into the system, improving its accuracy and decision-making capabilities over time.

While Tesla's progress in AI-powered self-driving cars is impressive, challenges remain. Regulatory hurdles, ethical considerations around liability in accidents, and the complexity of handling unpredictable situations like adverse weather conditions are ongoing issues. However, with Tesla's commitment to innovation and its ever-evolving AI technology, we can expect continued advancements in the field. The ultimate goal of a truly autonomous and universally safe driving experience remains within reach, as predicted in the last chapter.

IBM

With IBM's AI-supercharged cloud computing, the days of manually sifting through massive amounts of data are a thing of the past. This technology enables lightning-fast and efficient data analysis. IBM's AI-driven analytics tools automate the process, uncovering hidden patterns, trends, and correlations that human eyes might miss. Insights into customer behavior, market dynamics, and operational efficiency become readily available, empowering data-driven decision-making.

Additionally, IBM provides a toolbox of pre-trained ML models and customizable tools that businesses can readily deploy to tackle specific challenges. From predicting equipment failures to optimizing marketing campaigns, ML becomes accessible and impactful, even for organizations with limited data science expertise. IBM's NLP services enable businesses to interact with customers through chatbots, analyze social media sentiments, and even extract insights from textual documents, streamlining communication and unlocking valuable information.

Moreover, IBM's cognitive computer system, Watson, assists doctors in diagnosing diseases, analyzing medical images, and even suggesting personalized treatment plans. Its ability to process vast amounts of medical data opens doors to faster diagnoses, improved treatment outcomes, and personalized healthcare experiences. From analyzing market trends to predicting customer churn, Watson also empowers businesses with advanced decision-making tools. By understanding customer behavior and anticipating market shifts, companies can optimize their strategies, resources, and overall performance.

IBM does not stop at Watson. Its cloud platform offers a diverse range of AI solutions addressing various needs. Speech recognition, visual recognition, and fraud detection are just a few examples of how IBM empowers businesses to overcome complex challenges through the power of AI. IBM's cloud-based AI solutions pave the way for a future where businesses of all sizes can leverage the power of AI. Improved efficiency, data-driven decisions, and innovative solutions become accessible, fostering growth and progress across various industries. As AI technology continues to evolve, IBM's commitment to providing accessible and versatile tools ensures businesses remain at the forefront of this transformative era.

Meta Platforms

While Meta Platforms dominates the social media landscape with Facebook, Instagram, WhatsApp, and lately, Threads, it is no stranger to the world of AI. In fact, AI permeates its products and services in a multitude of ways, far beyond simply powering recommendation algorithms. AI fuels those meticulously curated feeds you see on Facebook and Instagram. Analyzing your past clicks, interactions, and even inferred interests, AI algorithms recommend accounts, groups, and content, keeping you hooked and engaged.

Moreover, identifying potentially harmful content like hate speech or nudity is crucial for maintaining a safe online environment. Meta leverages AI for image and text recognition, automatically flagging such content for review and removal. Chatbots powered by AI handle customer inquiries on various platforms, providing instant support and freeing up human resources. Meanwhile, virtual assistants like Meta Assistant offer hands-free control over your digital world, and real-time translation breaks down language barriers, fostering global connections.

These are just a few examples of how Meta Platforms harnesses the power of AI. From shaping your online experience to enhancing accessibility and bridging communication gaps, AI is woven into the very fabric of its platform, pushing the boundaries of what is possible and shaping the future of social media and beyond.

Boeing

Boeing's collaboration with Shield AI, a leader in autonomous flight technology, marks a bold step towards self-piloting aircraft. Shield AI's AI pilot, Hivemind, has already proven its mettle by flying fighter jets, drones, and other diverse aircraft, paving the way for a future where human hands may eventually give way to intelligent algorithms in the cockpit. The potential goes beyond a single aircraft. Hivemind's ability to enable autonomous drone and aircraft operations opens doors to new possibilities in logistics, surveillance, and even disaster response. Imagine fleets of intelligent drones coordinating seamlessly to deliver vital supplies or map disaster zones, all piloted by the power of AI. Boeing is also actively experimenting with AI-powered air traffic management systems. Advanced CV algorithms can analyze real-time data from aircraft transponders and radar, optimizing flight paths, preventing collisions, and ensuring smoother, more efficient air travel. This could significantly reduce delays and congestion, making the skies a more predictable and sustainable playground.

Furthermore, speech recognition technology finds its place in the air traffic control tower. AI systems can interpret pilot reports and instructions with unparalleled accuracy, reducing the risk of miscommunication and enhancing safety at a crucial stage of the flight. The same applies with image recognition features: Imagine landing an aircraft only to have AI instantly analyze high-resolution pictures of every inch of its exterior, spotting even the most minute cracks or dents. This is the vision Boeing pursues with its AI-powered image analysis technology. By automating and streamlining the inspection process, AI minimizes downtime, bolsters safety, and ensures planes are always flight-worthy.

The power of AI goes beyond mere damage detection. By analyzing past inspection data and aircraft performance metrics, AI algorithms can predict potential failures before they occur, allowing for proactive maintenance and preventing costly breakdowns. This predictive approach optimizes maintenance schedules, reduces risk, and keeps planes operational longer. Boeing's embrace of AI showcases the transformative potential of this technology in the aerospace industry. From autonomous flight to intelligent air traffic management and AI-powered inspections, the future of aviation promises to be shaped by the seamless collaboration between human innovation and machine intelligence.

J.P. Morgan Chase

While Silicon Valley giants dominate the headlines with their AI advancements, a silent revolution is brewing in the heart of finance. Wall Street whales like J.P. Morgan Chase are quietly harnessing the potential of AI, transforming banking from the inside out. JPM's AI-powered fraud detection systems work with algorithmic precision. Imagine an army of tireless sentinels, constantly analyzing millions of transactions for anomalies. By learning from past attacks and identifying suspicious patterns in real-time, these algorithms nip fraud in the bud, protecting both the bank and its customers. JPM is also exploring AI that understands user intent and adapts its responses, offering personalized assistance and proactive solutions. This emotional intelligence elevates customer service, building trust and loyalty in a complex and often-opaque industry.

Things get truly fascinating as JPM's embrace of LLMs, like ChatGPT, goes beyond chatbots. They are using it to analyze decades of Federal Reserve speeches, dissecting the nuances of language and extracting potential trading signals. Imagine gaining an edge by anticipating the market's reaction to every subtle inflection in a chairman's address! Beyond this innovative experiment, JPM, like many financial giants, utilizes well-established AI methods like algorithmic trading. These automated systems, powered by complex algorithms, analyze market data and execute trades at lightning speed, optimizing returns and managing risk with exceptional efficiency.

Furthermore, JPM's foray into AI paints a vivid picture of the future of finance. Humans and machines will work in tandem, leveraging each other's strengths. The creativity and strategic vision of humans will be amplified by the analytical power and tireless execution of AI, resulting in smarter risk management, personalized customer experiences, and even the ability to anticipate market whispers. This is just one glimpse into the transformative power of AI in finance. As technology evolves and regulations adapt, financial institutions like JPM will continue to push the boundaries, shaping a future where data-driven insights and algorithmic partners empower them to navigate the ever-changing market landscape with unparalleled finesse.

In light of these practical steps to implementing AI, as demon-strated by the above pathfinders, I hope you get the gist of this technology's potential to revolutionize the way your business operates. The few succeeding chapters dive deeper into specific business operations, starting with AI in customer relations management.

EMPOWERING BUSINESS LEADERS

"Knowledge is like money: To be of value it must circulate, and in circulating it can increase in quantity and, hopefully, in value."

— LOUIS L'AMOUR

If I had been less resistant to AI and embraced the possibilities it offers sooner, my business would have become successful much more quickly. I'd been put off by ethical horror stories, and I wasn't convinced that it was more than a passing phase, one I expected to slip away as quickly as it had come on the scene.

It took me a long time to realize that AI was a tool—and like any tool, its success depends on how well you use it. It's because I realized how much I had missed out on because of my hesitation that I decided to write this book. The business world can't afford to let AI slip by as forward-thinking companies pick it up and take their work to the next level. We need an even playing field, and that means that it's fair for everyone to be able to harness the powers of AI with care and wisdom.

So, in the spirit of leveling that playing field, I'd like to ask for your help. If you would be willing to leave your feedback online, you'd not only help me improve this resource for future readers but also help other business leaders find everything they need to make AI work for them.

By leaving a review of this book on Amazon, you'll highlight the power of AI in business and help new readers find the guidance they need to use it efficiently.

There's a lot of noise about AI out there, and it's muddying the waters. By clearly signposting where the helpful information is, we can help business owners to use it to step into the future.

Thank you so much for your support. There's so much misunderstanding about AI out there, and our businesses can't afford for us to miss out.

6

ARTIFICIAL INTELLIGENCE IN CUSTOMER RELATIONSHIP MANAGEMENT

A I is not just about automation; it is about leveraging data and technology to deliver a more human-centric customer experience. By using it strategically, businesses can create personalized interactions, anticipate needs, address concerns proactively, and build stronger relationships with their customers. This chapter offers more insight on how AI enhances the customer experience using different AI-powered CRM platforms.

HOW AI CAN ENHANCE CUSTOMER EXPERIENCE AND ENGAGEMENT

Imagine a bustling shopping mall where friendly robots greet you, curate personalized shopping recommendations, and answer your questions with instant expertise. That is just a glimpse of how AI can transform the customer experience and engagement.

Personalizing Customer Interactions

Imagine entering a coffee shop where the barista greets you by name and suggests your usual latte with extra cinnamon if it is a chilly day. You feel noticed and important because you are a valued regular customer in this place, which is why they remember how you like your coffee. As a result, you will probably buy your coffee nowhere else but here. That is how AI analyzes your purchase history and preferences to create a personal touch. You can see this when an online clothing store recommends outfits based on your browsing history and past purchases, like a virtual stylist who knows your taste and size perfectly.

AI analyzes customer purchase history, browsing behavior, and even social media data to suggest products they would genuinely love, just like a virtual personal shopper who truly understands your taste. Websites and apps also adapt their content and offers based on your individual preferences, making interactions feel like a tailored conversation, not a generic sales pitch. You can see the effectiveness of personalized customer interactions with behemoth companies like Netflix. It recommends new shows based on your viewing habits and alerts you when new seasons of your favorites are released. That is why it has a record of customers who feel valued and understood, leading to increased loyalty and brand affinity. The more customers stream shows and never miss a subscription, the more money Netflix makes. These are the main benefits that any company using AI can expect.

Providing Proactive Customer Support

AI can predict customers' potential needs and offer solutions before issues arise. Imagine receiving a text message from your airline before your flight reminding you to check in online and suggesting nearby restaurants at your destination. Automatically, you are saved from being late for your flight or having to manually check places to unwind and eat. Customers appreciate the anticipation and feel cared for, reducing frustration and enhancing satisfaction.

Automating Customer Service Tasks

AI-powered chatbots provide 24/7 instant support that answers basic questions, resolves simple issues, and seamlessly hands over complex ones to human agents. Customers do not have to wait for your company's operating hours or for the next available agent, who may currently be preoccupied with other responsibilities. AI chatbots provide immediate support, answering basic questions like order status, product details, or return policies in a flash. This instant gratification keeps customers satisfied and reduces frustration, especially in a world where patience is often a scarce commodity.

Developing Targeted Marketing Campaigns

Targeted marketing campaigns ensure that customers receive relevant offers that genuinely interest them, increasing conversion rates and brand engagement. Imagine receiving personalized discount codes for products you were browsing online or emails with promotional offers tailored to your interests, like secret invitations to exclusive sales. This could help businesses create on-point marketing ads that directly communicate with relevant customers instead of throwing a needle in a haystack and hoping someone finds it.

Analyzing Customer Feedback

AI analyzes customer reviews and social media conversations to understand their emotions and identify areas for improvement, allowing you to address concerns and nurture loyalty. For example, a restaurant could use AI to analyze customer feedback on its new menu and identify the least popular dishes, prompting them to make adjustments, like a wise chef constantly improving their recipes based on diner feedback. This could help businesses gain valuable insights to improve their products and services, leading to higher customer satisfaction and loyalty.

CASE STUDIES OF SUCCESSFUL AI-DRIVEN CRM APPLICATIONS

Learning from those with a record of success can be inspiring. As you navigate through the following AI-powered CRM platforms, consider your business needs, specific goals, and budget. Some platforms cater to specific industries and offer features tailored to their challenges and workflows. The good thing is that most platforms offer free trials or demos, allowing you to test drive the software and see if it fits your needs.

Salesforce Einstein CRM Platform

Salesforce integrates AI through its Einstein CRM platform, a robust solution designed to enhance CRM. Einstein CRM automates routine customer service tasks, streamlining processes and allowing service teams to focus on more complex issues. It performs lead scoring by analyzing the leads that are likely to convert into sales. It does this by analyzing how customers are likely to engage with your leads or content based on their previous behavior with similar content. Additionally, Einstein CRM helps businesses develop targeted marketing campaigns by analyzing customer data, predicting trends, and recommending strategies for effective outreach. Einstein CRM is a great example demonstrating how AI-driven insights enable businesses to personalize customer interactions. This personalization spans from tailored communication to recommending products or services based on customer preferences (Zhinko, 2018).

HubSpot

HubSpot incorporates AI into its Sales Hub CRM platform, offering powerful tools to manage leads, close deals, and boost sales pipelines. Some of the key aspects of HubSpot's AI integration include lead tracking, deal closure support, and sales pipeline growth. The AI-powered system assists businesses in tracking leads, providing insights into lead behavior, and predicting potential conversion opportunities. HubSpot's AI aids in identifying key factors influencing deal closures, allowing sales teams to focus efforts on promising opportunities. By leveraging AI insights, businesses can optimize their sales pipeline, making data-driven decisions for increased efficiency and revenue.

Moreover, HubSpot recently introduced two efficient AI tools into its system: HubSpot Content Assistant, which enables marketing and sales teams to brainstorm ideas, create, and share quality content in the blink of an eye. ChatSpot, on the other hand, is a conversational CRM bot connecting marketing, sales, and service professionals to HubSpot for maximum productivity. You can even boost your productivity by skipping the manual data entry on HubSpot and asking Chatspot to create content for you in a matter of minutes. ChatSpot can even send follow-up emails on your behalf, pull reports, and create new segments. Another upside is that HubSpot CRM offers a free basic plan, which makes it ideal for startups and small businesses, offering access to core CRM functionalities like contact management, email marketing, and sales pipeline tracking (Business Solution, 2023).

Zoho CRM

Zoho CRM incorporates AI through its Zia assistant, offering intelligent automation and support. Zia assists businesses by automating tasks, reducing manual workload, and improving overall operational efficiency. Furthermore, Zia is designed to answer queries, providing valuable information and insights to users based on the data within the CRM system. The AI capabilities of Zoho CRM extend to generating insights from data, helping businesses make informed decisions and identify trends. Zoho has a range of other applications for their CRM customers. These include projects, campaigns, mail, surveys, desks, and financial suites. Another great feature of Zoho CRM is its ability to be integrated with other third parties, allowing its users to link productivity tools like Google, Microsoft, social media, and other CRMs like Salesforce and HubSpot. This makes data synchronization possible and smooth (Caballero, 2023).

Freshsales

Freshsales CRM has an efficient AI-powered chatbot, Freddy AI, which engages leads, answers customer questions, and schedules appointments, improving lead conversion and customer satisfaction. With its ability to focus on sales automation, it streamlines workflows with auto-escalation rules, email sequencing, and predictive lead scoring. Freshsales CRM is also user-friendly and easy to navigate, making it suitable for teams with varying levels of technical expertise.

ActiveCampaign

ActiveCampaign uses AI to create automated email sequences and personalized marketing campaigns based on customer behavior and preferences. It automates repetitive tasks like social media engagement, lead nurturing, and customer segmentation. Furthermore, ActiveCampaign provides a comprehensive marketing suite that combines CRM functionalities with email marketing, marketing automation, and analytics tools for a unified marketing approach.

LivePerson

LivePerson's AI-powered conversational platform revolutionizes customer service by analyzing intent and emotions to guide conversations effectively. Its ability to handle multiple interactions simultaneously, whether through human agents, bots, or integrations, ensures seamless customer interactions while reducing operational costs. This intelligent platform paves the way for personalized and efficient customer service experiences.

BENEFITS

AI offers a landscape of benefits for helping businesses handle customer relations. Leveraging AI in CRM offers a potent blend of efficiency, personalization, and valuable insights. Businesses can harness the power of AI in CRM to enhance customer relationships and achieve sustainable growth.

Personalized Experiences

AI analyzes customer data, preferences, and interactions to predict needs and deliver personalized experiences. Imagine chatbots anticipating questions, suggesting relevant products, and tailoring communication styles to individual preferences. This fosters positive emotions, builds loyalty, and increases overall satisfaction.

Increased Sales

AI-driven insights help sales teams identify potential leads more accurately and prioritize high-value opportunities. It enables sales teams to engage with customers in a more targeted and effective manner, improving conversion rates.

Enhanced Efficiency and Automation

AI automates repetitive tasks like data entry, scheduling appointments, and routing inquiries. This frees up human agents to focus on complex issues and high-value interactions, ultimately improving efficiency and cost-effectiveness. It also enhances the speed and accuracy of data analysis, providing real-time insights for better decision support. Automation of routine tasks in CRM processes through AI also reduces the need for manual labor and human error, leading to cost savings. This streamlines operations and resource allocation, optimizing overall efficiency.

Predictive Analytics and Insights

AI algorithms analyze data patterns to anticipate customer churn, identify potential issues, and predict future needs. This empowers businesses to proactively address problems, offer targeted solutions, and prevent churn before it happens.

24/7 Availability and Support

AI-powered chatbots and virtual assistants can provide 24/7 support, answer basic questions, and resolve simple issues. This ensures constant customer attention and reduces reliance on human agents during off-peak hours.

Data-Driven Decision Making

AI analyzes customer interactions and feedback to provide valuable insights into customer preferences, trends, and sentiment. This data-driven approach empowers businesses to make informed decisions about product development, marketing strategies, and overall customer experience improvements.

CHALLENGES

While the potential benefits are vast, integrating AI also presents a unique set of challenges. It is crucial to understand the shortcomings of implementing AI in CRM in order to understand how to overcome these limitations.

High Initial Costs

Implementing AI in CRM systems can involve significant upfront costs, including technology acquisition, training, and maintenance. The initial investment in AI technology can be hefty, encompassing software licenses, hardware upgrades, and expert consultation. Companies need to consider the costs of acquisition, deployment, and ongoing maintenance before taking the plunge. Beyond the upfront price tag, hidden costs like data storage, training programs, and potential compatibility issues with existing infrastructure can emerge. Therefore, thorough planning and cost-benefit analysis are crucial to avoid financial surprises down the line.

Complexity

The technical complexity of AI systems may require specialized skills for implementation and management. Recruiting or upskilling talent to handle this complexity can be a hurdle for some businesses. Moreover, integrating AI seamlessly with existing CRM infrastructure can pose challenges, potentially causing disruptions. Data formats, communication protocols, and security measures may clash, leading to compatibility issues and operational disruptions. Some AI models can be opaque and complex, making it difficult to understand how they arrive at decisions. This lack of transparency can raise concerns about bias and fairness in customer interactions, eroding trust and hindering accountability.

Data Privacy and Security

Integrating AI necessitates collecting and analyzing vast amounts of customer data. This raises concerns about data privacy, security, and potential misuse. Businesses need to ensure transparency, secure data storage, and clear communication with customers about data usage.

Ethical Considerations and Bias

AI algorithms can perpetuate biases present in the data they are trained on. This can lead to discriminatory practices and unfair treatment of certain customer segments. Businesses must actively monitor and address potential biases to ensure the ethical and equitable application of AI in CRM.

Job Displacement Fears

Automation through AI can lead to job displacement in customer service roles. Businesses need to implement AI responsibly, focusing on tasks that complement human agents rather than replacing them altogether. Continuous training and upskilling initiatives are crucial to adapting the workforce to the changing dynamics of AI-powered CRM.

Lack of Transparency and Explainability

As I mentioned earlier, some AI models can be complex and opaque, making it difficult to understand how they arrive at certain decisions. This lack of transparency can erode customer trust and hinder effective complaint resolution. Businesses need to strive for transparent AI models and provide clear explanations for their decisions to maintain customer confidence.

Human Touch Dilemma

While AI can streamline processes and provide efficient support, human interaction remains irreplaceable for complex issues, emotional situations, and building genuine relationships with customers. Finding the right balance between AI efficiency and the human touch is crucial for delivering exceptional customer experiences.

Leveraging AI in CRM offers a potent blend of efficiency, personalization, and valuable insights. However, navigating the challenges around data privacy, bias, job displacement, and a lack of human connection is crucial for responsible and effective implementation. By embracing a human-centric approach and prioritizing data security and ethical considerations, businesses can harness the power of AI to revolutionize customer relations management and create truly exceptional customer experiences. The next chapter focuses on AI in data analytics.

7

ARTIFICIAL INTELLIGENCE IN DATA ANALYTICS AND INSIGHTS

According to recent findings, a substantial portion of businesses are leveraging AI to maximize the potential of their big data. In fact, a staggering 48% of organizations are utilizing some form of AI to effectively analyze and make decisions based on their large datasets (Howarth, 2023). Gone are the days when data analytics and insights strictly required business owners to pay premium rates to secure professional data scientists and analysts. While AI models may still have limitations when handling sensitive data, there are some basic analytic jobs that they can perform with little to no human intervention. Using real-world examples, this chapter sheds more light on the impact of AI in data analytics as well as how businesses can cautiously implement AI, knowing its shortcomings.

LEVERAGING AI FOR DATA ANALYSIS, PREDICTIVE MODELING, AND PATTERN RECOGNITION

With unique capabilities to analyze data, predict consumer behavior, forecast future outcomes, and recognize patterns, AI stands out as a technology every business can benefit from. This section provides insight on how AI-powered data analysts are structured and can be leveraged in various business departments.

Data Analysis

AI automates tedious tasks, uncovers hidden insights, and makes data accessible. Sometimes data requires proper structuring, cleaning, and preparation before it is presented to relevant departments. AI-powered tools like DataRobot streamline data cleaning, formatting, and standardization, saving time and reducing errors. Moreover, ML algorithms in tools like Tableau suggest relevant charts and visualizations, accelerating pattern discovery. Through NLP abilities, AI extracts insights from text data, enabling analysis of customer feedback, social media conversations, and internal documents. AI also pinpoints unusual patterns that might signal fraud, errors, or system failures, protecting businesses from losses and disruptions.

Predictive Modeling

AI builds models that forecast future outcomes based on historical patterns. AI predicts customer churn, product preferences, and purchase likelihood, enabling proactive retention strategies and personalized recommendations, as seen with Amazon and Netflix in previous examples. Additionally, it predicts sales trends, inventory needs, and resource allocation, improving supply chain management and reducing costs. Walmart and Target use this information to keep their inventories stocked to meet consumer demands. AI models assess credit risk for financial institutions, predict equipment failures for manufacturing, and identify potential healthcare complications for patients.

Pattern Recognition

AI excels at recognizing patterns within complex data. It powers facial recognition, object detection in autonomous vehicles, and medical image analysis. The AI speech recognition technique also enables voice assistants like Siri and Alexa, transcribes audio recordings, and translates languages in real-time. Furthermore, AI uses its fraud detection ability to identify fraudulent transactions, insurance claims, and online scams, protecting organizations and individuals from financial losses. It also groups customers based on shared characteristics and behaviors, enabling targeted marketing campaigns and personalized experiences.

REAL-WORLD EXAMPLES OF AI-POWERED DATA ANALYTICS SOLUTIONS

Using AI in data analytics solutions may be one of the groundbreaking successes of this revolutionary technology. From generating and editing code to fixing bug issues and creating automated data reports, AI can be seen as a star simplifying the job of data scientists and analysts. For minor applications, even people with no experience in this field can deploy some AI tools to handle non-sensitive analytical data. This section succinctly depicts real-world examples of AI integration in solution-based data analytics and insights.

Generating Code and Debugging Errors

It is no secret that coding is complex work reserved for computer scientists and technology nerds. However, because of AI, the playing field has been leveled. While not everyone can code or debug code-related errors, AI coding assistants act as tireless programmers, writing code, catching bugs, and suggesting improvements. This increases productivity, reduces errors, and improves code quality, enabling faster development of data analytics solutions. We will look at how this simplifies the work of professional coders, programmers, and data scientists in the following examples:

- DataCamp Workspace AI automatically suggests code snippets, simplifies debugging, and personalizes learning paths for data scientists.
- Anaconda Assistant helps users navigate libraries, find relevant functions, and write more efficient code.
- Jupyter AI offers code completion, intelligent insights, and debugging assistance within Jupyter Notebooks.
- GitHub Copilot generates code suggestions based on context and user preferences, accelerating development cycles.

Creating Synthetic Data

You may recall that one of the challenges most companies face in implementing AI is a lack of real data to train models on. Advanced AI solutions are able to solve this problem by generating realistic and diverse data to train models, protect privacy, and overcome data scarcity. A great benefit of using synthetic data is privacy protection, as no real data is used. This overcomes data privacy concerns, enables model development in restricted domains, and enhances model accuracy. For instance, if there is limited or sensitive data to diagnose certain diseases, AI can create synthetic data. The Gartner report even predicts that future AI models will be mainly trained on synthetic data by 2030 (Ramos, 2023). This plan is already in motion, as can be seen in the following applications:

- AI can be used to create simulations for testing and experimentation used in financial modeling.
- Image recognition also helps augment existing datasets to improve model performance.

Creating Dashboards and Reports

Several AI tools can now process and analyze data from images. Additionally, AI automates the creation of insightful and visually appealing dashboards, saving time and effort. Faster and more efficient reporting, enabling better communication of insights to stakeholders, and driving data-driven decision-making. Even without any prior experience in data visualization, you can command AI to include a particular image or visualization in your presentation, and it will format it accordingly.

- Tableau GPT automatically generates dashboards from natural language queries, incorporating visualizations and insights relevant to specific questions.
- MidJourney also allows you to generate some eye-catching images that you can incorporate into your data analysis reports.

Explaining Analysis and Insights

AI transforms data into understandable stories, revealing hidden patterns and making insights accessible to everyone. Analytical data is often full of charts, graphs, and reports that are hard to comprehend by non-technical users. Even if you were to check your post analytics, there are cryptic insights that need someone well-versed in numbers and data science. AI tools like Tableau GPT explain data in a simplified manner. Tableau GPT provides natural language explanations for visual analysis, answering questions like "Why is this sales trend occurring?" or "What factors are influencing customer churn?" in simple terms. An enhanced understanding of data leads to better collaboration and wiser decision-making.

THE SIGNIFICANT AI CONTRIBUTION IN DATA ANALYTICS

In the ever-expanding landscape of data analytics, AI stands as a transformative force, reshaping how organizations glean insights from vast and complex datasets. AI brings a unique set of capabilities to the realm of data analysis, ranging from predictive modeling and anomaly detection to automated data preparation and intelligent insights. This section explores the profound significance of AI in data analytics, unraveling the ways in which smart algorithms, NLP, and ML empower businesses to extract meaningful patterns, predict trends, and make informed decisions in the dynamic world of big data.

Anomaly Detection

As technology advances, so do bad actors, leading to data theft and discrepancies. AI acts as a vigilant security guard, spotting unusual patterns that might signal fraud, errors, or system failures. Early identification of anomalies can prevent significant financial losses, reputational damage, and operational disruptions. For instance, PayPal uses AI to detect fraudulent transactions in real-time, protecting both buyers and sellers from financial losses. This would lead to significant losses if humans were entrusted with this responsibility because it would take them longer to detect fraudulent activities. In most cases, by the time manual anomaly detection reveals any danger, the most damage has already been done.

Data-Driven Predictive Analytics

We have already established that predictive analytics enables AI to peer into the future, making informed predictions about customer behavior, sales trends, or resource needs. This helps any business create, market, and sell relevant products that customers are already interested in. On the other hand, manually analyzing this data could take a lot of time for your team of data scientists. But with AI, you can have improved decision-making, proactive planning, and optimization of resources across various business functions.

Automated Data Cleaning and Preparation

AI serves like a meticulous librarian, organizing messy data into clean, usable formats, saving time, and ensuring accuracy. Faster, more accurate data analysis leads to better insights and a reduced risk of errors. Data preparation tools like DataRobot automate the cleaning, formatting, and standardization of datasets, reducing manual effort and accelerating analysis. AI also automates report generation after any analysis has been completed, freeing your team from manually creating individual reports.

Data Democratization

Using NLP, AI unlocks the meaning within text data, extracting insights from customer reviews, social media posts, emails, and more. This makes data accessible and usable to more people within your team, instead of limiting data understanding to data analysts only. Data democratization leads to a deeper understanding of customer sentiment, market trends, and brand reputation, enabling data-driven decision-making for everyone within the team. For example, sentiment analysis tools like MonkeyLearn analyze customer feedback to gauge satisfaction levels and identify areas for improvement.

ML-Powered Data Exploration

AI acts as a tireless explorer, uncovering hidden patterns and relationships within large datasets that humans might miss. The accelerated discovery of valuable insights leads to innovative strategies and solutions. Data visualization platforms like Tableau leverage ML to suggest relevant charts and visualizations, revealing insights quickly.

AI-Powered Business Intelligence Tools

AI-infused BI platforms offer intelligent insights and recommendations, guiding decision-making. One such tool is Qlik Sense, which incorporates AI to deliver personalized insights, predictive analytics, and natural language querying capabilities. Instead of just showing you the data as it is, it also demonstrates how it understands it and ensures that you do too. Domo's AI-powered Business Dashboard is another BI tool designed to grow alongside your company, seamlessly integrating with popular applications such as Salesforce, Square, Facebook, and Shopify to provide a comprehensive view of your customers, sales performance, and inventory management. With this innovative solution, you can gain valuable insights and make data-driven decisions to drive your business forward.

LIMITATIONS OF AI IN DATA ANALYTICS

While the information above demonstrates the invaluable capabilities of AI in analyzing complex data and doing the greater part of the job of data analysts and scientists, it has its limitations. It is important to understand how limited AI is to avoid its extensive implementation in areas where it could provide false data and cause great harm. Before you fire your data analyst because you found the perfect AI-powered data analytics tool, consider the following ways in which AI falls short:

Hallucinations

We can attest that sometimes AI lacks explainability, whereby it can respond to commands and provide solutions without fully disclosing its methods or how it reached a particular result. Although AI is known to bring the correct information, a human must still verify that that information contains no errors. When faced with complex data, AI has the tendency to hallucinate or make stuff up that is most likely to be the answer, although it may be wrong. Even though it will perform its tasks and analyze given data, it will not always reveal that the information is inaccurate. Validating this information can be a challenge for someone who lacks a basic understanding of data analytics.

Blind Spots

Blind spots are cases where AI finds it harder to perform given tasks in a certain way than it prefers. You may have heard that a machine's efficiency lies with the user. You can have a tool perform below its maximum capabilities if you only have basic and moderate knowledge. Unless you know how to identify and rectify a limited device, you can be convinced that it cannot perform beyond what you are asking for and settle for mediocre results. Sometimes AI gets stuck on very basic questions if the prompt is unclear or too complex. Giving a coding prompt can be complicated for a non-techy user. AI can get stuck explaining certain queries or fail to reason in an understandable manner. Even if you point out its mistake, it can still repeat itself in a new result because it has reached a blind spot. You can spend your entire time trying to change your prompt or make an AI model realize This can be frustrating without a human data scientist or analyst. In fact, a human analyst would be more open to correction and seek external help until they found a satisfactory solution.

Humble Experts

Have you ever asked ChatGPT or any AI tool to perform a certain task and told it that you were unhappy with the result? Even if you are the one who gave it an incomplete or unclear prompt, the AI model is trained to admit the fault as its own and try to give an alternative response. AI tends to agree with you even if you are wrong because it is trained to obey commands and be a humble expert. This is not the case in the business world; if you hire an expert, they are not afraid to put you in your place, where you are an amateur when it comes to their field. They tell you straight up that you are wrong and show you the right way something is supposed to be. This makes AI data analysis questionable because the results are based on how firm the person who gave it the prompt was.

Token Limit

Human data analysts work until they find a solution to a problem, no matter how long it takes. This means they can take months to work on an extensive project, gather vast amounts of data, and produce a comprehensive report without saying it is too much. However, AI models have a limit on their data input and output. If you input a query beyond the AI's token limit, it will respond that you need to shorten it first. For instance, most free versions of AI tools basically have a token limit of around 10,000 words, or 15,000 characters. The paid version of ChatGPT-4 has a limit of 12 pages. If your data requires an input length longer than this, a human data analyst is your only option (Mulli, 2023).

Lack of Personal Touch

An AI data analyst will often work on given data only, while a human data analyst can look at relational data beyond company records. Some reports can be analyzed and shook on based on personal relationships and counter-deals. Human interaction is important during data projects. AI models, on the other hand, only focus on what is in front of them, with no ability to read non-verbal communication or interpret personal touch that could potentially move the project further.

Challenges in Updating Business Data

Every business has its own data model with columns and values that may have different meanings in other companies' databases. Even if an AI model can analyze data, it might do so with a different interpretation. A human data analyst will still be required to ensure that the AI model understands the company database. They must also keep it updated in such a way that the people using that data are kept in the loop.

Data analytics and insights often require expert data scientists and analysts to interpret company reports and keep databases updated. AI is now proving its efficiency in simplifying things for businesses that want to avoid paying premium rates to book professional analysts. While some of the AI models discussed in this chapter are competent, it is important to note that AI is still in its infancy and has some limitations. Therefore, sensitive business information still requires human data analysts. Perhaps this indicates that AI is far from replacing humans; instead, it is here to make human-machine collaboration a formidable team. The following chapter discusses the implementation of AI in marketing and sales.

8

ARTIFICIAL INTELLIGENCE IN MARKETING AND SALES

A I has transformed the way businesses approach marketing and sales, moving away from intuition and manual effort to data-driven strategies that are highly personalized and precise. This shift has the potential to revolutionize the way companies engage with their customers, moving beyond broad, generic campaigns to hyper-personalized approaches that cater to individual preferences and behaviors. This chapter sheds more light on the behind-the-scenes approach to how AI is making strides in this industry, not forgetting that sales are the bloodline of every business.

HOW AI CAN OPTIMIZE MARKETING CAMPAIGNS AND SALES STRATEGIES

In this digital age, businesses can optimize marketing campaigns and refine sales strategies using the power of AI. Unlocking the vast AI potential helps them achieve sustainable growth. From personalized marketing to automated marketing tasks, AI is bringing a paradigm shift into this industry, helping businesses maximize their profits while saving more time.

Personalizing Marketing Messages

While the aim of marketing is to reach out to clients to ignite a sale, there are several ways to avoid direct selling, which can be annoying and less effective. Sending your customers communicative and meaningful messages can be more effective than showcasing a new product with a direct call to action for them to buy. Imagine sending birthday greetings with personalized product recommendations to each customer, not generic emails. AI analyzes purchase history, interests, and online behavior to craft tailor-made messages that resonate. The customer reads this personal note feeling like the universe is sending them a message. For example, Amazon uses AI to recommend products based on the customer's browsing history and past purchases, making them feel like they understand their needs. This leads to increased engagement because the customer may be tempted to click the link or view the attached product. Whether they end up buying the product themselves or sharing the link with their loved ones to consider gifting them, this interaction can lead to higher conversion rates and stronger customer relationships.

Targeting the Right Audience

When creating a marketing piece, it can be hard to tell who will react and how it communicates with them. Marketing is a fishing strategy to communicate your business message with the aim of hooking those who resonate with it. Finding the perfect audience for your product is like throwing the net into the water and withdrawing it with a great catch every time. AI analyzes vast datasets to identify ideal customer profiles based on demographics, interests, and online behavior. For instance, Facebook uses AI to target its ads at specific user groups, ensuring your message reaches the right people. Reaching your target audience reduces extensive advertising costs, improves campaign performance, and results in more qualified leads.

Generating Leads

Imagine having a tireless AI assistant find potential customers 24/7. AI-powered chatbots engage website visitors, answer questions, and capture leads even when you are sleeping. Many airlines use chatbots to answer travel questions and help customers book flights, simplifying the buying journey. This increases lead generation, maintains 24/7 customer service, and improves the user experience.

Automating Marketing Tasks

We have already established that freeing up your time for strategic planning while AI handles the mundane is the gist behind task automation and the greater reason for increased AI adoption. AI automates repetitive tasks like email scheduling, social media posting, and data analysis. For example, Hootsuite allows you to schedule social media posts in advance, saving valuable time for content creation and engagement. You can use AI to analyze the time when your posts get more impressions so that you can schedule your future posts to publish at the same time, even if you are engaged with other tasks. This consistency will help grow your audience, as your followers will know that your posts are always on time. Automating email scheduling also ensures that you send emails around the time when your recipients are more likely to read and engage with your message. This increases efficiency, reduces operational costs, and frees up more time for strategic initiatives.

Measuring and Optimizing Marketing Performance

It can be challenging to understand what works and what does not, especially if you do not have time to check the data analytics of your marketing campaigns. Thankfully, AI analyzes campaign data to identify successes and failures, allowing for continuous optimization. For instance, Google Analytics provides detailed insights into website traffic, helping you understand how visitors interact with your content. Using AI tools to optimize your marketing performance leads to data-driven decision-making, improved campaign performance, and a higher ROI.

PERSONALIZATION, TARGETED ADVERTISING, AND LEAD GENERATION USING AI

AI transforms personalization, targeted advertising, and lead generation into dynamic, data-driven processes. By harnessing the power of AI, businesses can forge deeper connections with their audience, deliver more relevant and timely content, and streamline lead generation efforts for enhanced efficiency and conversion rates.

Analyzing Customer Data

AI processes vast volumes of customer data, including demographics, behaviors, and preferences. Advanced AI algorithms identify patterns, uncovering valuable insights into customer interactions, purchasing history, and engagement levels. By analyzing historical data, AI uncovers trends and preferences, laying the foundation for personalized strategies. If you know your customer's preferences and behavior, it should not be hard to determine what they are most likely to purchase. Remember the Amazon example mentioned several times? Browsing history can be a great indication of what they will purchase next.

Identifying Customer Segments

AI algorithms categorize customers into segments based on shared characteristics and behaviors. For instance, you can group your customers based on their spending habits and product interests. While AI enables you to treat each customer as an individual through personalized marketing, it also helps to identify like-minded and congregation-like audiences that resonate with the same message and react similarly. You can save money by creating an ad that will reach a particular group of people at once, rather than creating multiple ads to fit each customer. This means that you can have different pricing strategies for each group of people, knowing that you are likely to make a sale regardless of your offer. You can channel low-ticket offers to the conservative group and medium- to high-ticket offers to the big spenders' group. AI also helps save time by sending a generic message to a particular customer segment, although it still contains personal touches like a customer's first name. Additionally, continuous learning enables AI to adapt segmentation in real-time, ensuring relevance as customer behaviors evolve. Fine-grained segmentation also allows for highly targeted approaches, tailoring strategies to specific customer subgroups.

Developing Targeted Marketing Campaigns

With AI, you can ditch the generic "Dear valued customer" emails. Leveraging customer insights, AI generates personalized content that resonates with individual preferences. AI determines the most effective channels for communication based on historical responses and real-time engagement. For instance, some customers may engage more with your Instagram content than they do on Facebook or in emails. AI allows you to reach out to individual customers through their preferred means of communication. Furthermore, smart algorithms conduct A/B testing to refine campaign elements, optimizing messaging, visuals, and delivery methods.

Predicting Customer Behavior

With smart technologies like predictive analytics, foretelling what a customer is likely to do is possible. AI employs predictive models to forecast future customer behavior based on historical data. Knowing how a customer will engage, AI algorithms recommend products or services by anticipating customer needs, boosting cross-selling and upselling opportunities. AI predicts potential churn or loss of interest by identifying signs of disengagement, enabling proactive retention strategies.

Automating Lead Generation Tasks

Say goodbye to tedious lead scoring and spreadsheets! AI takes over with automation and precision, acting like a tireless analyst who delves into data to identify high-potential leads based on your customized criteria. It tracks online behavior like website visits, social media clicks, and digital footprints to pinpoint leads with strong purchase intent or intense engagement. AI does not stop there; it handles the entire lead nurturing process, delivering personalized content at the right moments and expertly guiding prospects through the sales funnel. With AI's help, you can focus on building relationships and converting those promising leads into loyal, long-term customers.

BENEFITS OF USING AI IN MARKETING AND SALES

From targeted ads that speak directly to the customer to following up on positive leads, AI algorithms are changing the marketing and sales landscapes. Rather than chasing an uncertain customer with a generic message, AI enables businesses to treat their prospects and customers like they are the only clients, making them feel special and understood. Using these predictive tools to secure new clients, businesses can focus more on serving existing clients to retain them.

Precision Targeting

Imagine being able to precisely target your marketing efforts at the customers most likely to convert, maximizing your return on investment (ROI). With AI, you can analyze vast amounts of data to uncover hidden insights and behaviors, allowing you to tailor your campaigns to individual preferences and needs. This personalization at scale creates a seamless and engaging customer experience, leading to increased brand loyalty and sales.

Task Automation

AI can also automate repetitive tasks, freeing up human resources for more strategic planning and creative work. By automating tasks like lead scoring—a tedious process of evaluating hundreds of prospects—social media management, and email marketing, you can increase efficiency and focus on tasks that drive growth. Imagine lead scoring done in a flash by AI. Or picture social media management churning out engaging content and responding to comments seamlessly, without human intervention. This is the magic of AI automation. Repetitive tasks are no longer time-consuming roadblocks, but opportunities to free up your team for strategic planning, creative brainstorming, and building meaningful customer relationships. Think of it as adding an army of tireless assistants to your team, each dedicated to eliminating the mundane and amplifying your human genius.

Predict Customer Behavior

AI algorithms can predict customer behavior and future trends, providing valuable insights for product development, campaign planning, and resource allocation. Therefore, you can forget relying on gut feelings and guesswork and let AI algorithms analyze vast amounts of data—purchase history, online behavior, social media preferences—to paint a precise picture of your customers' future actions. This allows you to anticipate their needs, target campaigns with laser-like precision, and develop products they crave before they even realize it. Imagine launching a personalized marketing campaign just as a customer starts researching a new product, or predicting upcoming service inquiries and proactively reaching out to prevent them. With AI foresight, you can stay ahead of the curve, navigate market shifts with agility, and ensure your business always hits the right note with your customers.

Enhanced Insights

Human minds process information linearly, often missing hidden connections and subtle patterns. AI, however, sees the unseen. It can provide enhanced insights by analyzing data from multiple sources and uncovering hidden patterns and relationships that human minds might miss. It analyzes data from diverse sources—website clicks, social media mentions, customer surveys—to uncover hidden correlations and trends that would remain invisible to us. This data-driven intelligence empowers you to make informed decisions, allocate resources efficiently, and optimize your strategy based on real-time feedback. Picture identifying which marketing channels yield the highest conversion rates, understanding why certain products resonate with specific customer segments, or predicting potential issues before they even emerge. With AI as your data whisperer, you can turn insights into action, fuel growth, and unlock the full potential of your business.

CHALLENGES OF USING AI IN MARKETING AND SALES

While AI has incredible benefits in marketing and sales, as discussed above, it also has challenges that limit its full integration. The goal is not to eliminate human marketers, and yet, some companies may feel obliged to scale down and remain with only efficient AI tools. The challenge is that AI models are not intuitive and often lack emotional intelligence and creativity, which are great skills humans possess.

Lack of Creativity

We have already established that current AI technologies are narrow. While they can analyze data and automate tasks efficiently, they often lack creativity and intuition. AI tools used for marketing may only focus on available data and not look at any external factors that may affect a product's sale. For example, AI can identify the best-selling areas and provide data on closing deals, but it cannot exactly tell why a particular area is experiencing low sales. You would have to gather feedback from prospects and customers or deploy a tailored AI model that monitors customer's behavior. Human marketers have an advantage in this regard, as they can use their intuition and common sense to study an area or undocumented data to come up with reasons why a certain product is not selling.

Bias and Inaccurate Content Concerns

As I mentioned in Chapter 4, AI's output is only as good as the data it is trained on, and if the data has discrepancies, AI may produce inaccurate or unfair predictions. This can lead to targeted ads that are unfair to certain groups. Human marketers are also emotionally intelligent, which enables them to identify and avoid sensitive information that may harm a particular group. Current AI models lack this skill and may lead marketing teams into ethics-related trouble.

Threaten Job Security

With AI algorithms able to monitor customer behavior and send targeted leads that are likely to convert into sales, where do they leave human marketers? If AI is potentially bringing in more leads and increasing sales, some organizations will likely want to scale down their teams and only leave a few people to close sales. This integration threatens the job security of people doing other roles like recruiting and following up with clients because AI does them efficiently in half the time, saving businesses chunks of money.

Implementing AI in marketing and sales enables businesses to create personalized campaigns that speak directly to the customer instead of generic ads targeted at anyone. Customers like to feel special and understood; curating your offers based on their recent searches and purchasing behavior is a guaranteed way to hook them. Take advantage of this information, follow giant companies already leveraging this feature, and watch endless activity on your sales funnels. The next chapter addresses another great AI integration geared toward customer satisfaction and increased sales: supply chain management.

9

ARTIFICIAL INTELLIGENCE IN SUPPLY CHAIN MANAGEMENT

T he unexpected global disruption brought by COVID-19 indicated the need for a better means of response to product demand, transportation, and task automation. The abrupt halt in production of non-essential goods and services, disruption of scheduled deliveries, and unattended inventories led to a loss of income for logistics companies and manufacturers through excessive inventory levels and dissatisfied customers. As if having spoiled goods was not enough, the enforced lockdown that prevented any movement also reflected badly on these companies, as customers' orders had to be cancelled at the eleventh hour. While AI was in place prior to the global pandemic, its demand in the supply chain skyrocketed during unprecedented times. Companies that responded swiftly to AI integration recovered fast, indicating the ability of AI to turn things around and prevent future problems. This chapter sheds more light on how using AI streamlines supply chain processes, with relevant examples of known companies benefiting from this technological shift.

USING AI TO STREAMLINE SUPPLY CHAIN PROCESSES AND IMPROVE EFFICIENCY

From predicting product demand to optimizing warehouse operations, AI has been the ultimate star in streamlining supply chain processes. Customers no longer have to wait indefinitely for their orders to be processed and their products delivered because AI algorithms predict demand, assist with timely production and dispatch, and ensure route optimization. Companies benefit from AI by matching demand with supply and avoiding excessive inventory that could result in losses. With satisfied customers and optimized production, it is no secret that companies that integrate AI into their supply chain processes pride themselves on enhanced efficiency and profitability. By employing AI in supply chain processes, businesses can achieve a more responsive and efficient supply chain, reducing costs, minimizing risks, and enhancing overall operational performance.

Forecasting Demand

AI utilizes advanced algorithms to analyze historical data, market trends, and consumer behavior to predict future demand accurately. Manually doing these tasks would take the supply chain teams ample time that they could be using to handle the next deliveries. AI-driven forecasting improves accuracy, reducing the likelihood of stockouts or excess inventory. A business is able to produce the exact amount of required products to meet the demand. Therefore, there will be no money lost in delayed deliveries that temper client loyalty or spoiled goods as a result of overproduction. Moreover, real-time adjustments based on changing market conditions enhance the adaptability of the supply chain. A supply chain that is able to adapt to changing market conditions ensures that the company remains profitable and relevant even in unprecedented times.

Optimizing Inventory Levels

AI algorithms continuously analyze demand forecasts, supplier lead times, and current inventory levels to determine optimal stock levels. Maintaining optimal inventory levels minimizes holding costs and the risk of overstock, improving overall cost efficiency. This also ensures that products are available when needed, preventing potential revenue loss and customer dissatisfaction.

Planning Transportation

Transporting goods as timely as possible is great for any business that wants to maintain great customer satisfaction. AI facilitates the efficient scheduling of transportation, including delivery and pick-up, by considering factors like route optimization, traffic conditions, and delivery windows. Optimized routes and schedules reduce fuel costs and transportation expenses. AI makes planning transportation fairly easy by ensuring that ordered products are always ready to dispatch and that there are on-time deliveries and pickups from relevant points, improving customer satisfaction and maintaining supply chain reliability.

Automating Logistics Tasks

AI automates various logistics tasks, such as order processing, warehouse management, and tracking shipments. There is a rise in autonomous mobile robots, which use a fusion of AI technologies like ML and CV to sense a need to pick, pack, seal, load, and dispatch products. These bots are able to work with minimal human intervention, enabling human workers to focus on more complex tasks. Automation also reduces manual errors and accelerates the speed of logistics processes. It also allows human resources to focus on strategic decision-making rather than mundane, routine tasks.

EXAMPLES OF AI APPLICATIONS IN SUPPLY CHAIN

Like with the previous chapters, there are industry pioneers paving the way by implementing AI in supply chain management. With over 70% of supply chain leaders predicted to integrate AI into their systems by 2025, the following list of companies is just the tip of the iceberg for what is to come (Champion, 2023).

Coupa

Coupa empowers logistics organizations with AI-driven decision-making tools like the Supply Chain Modeler. It analyzes data, forecasts future scenarios, and factors in external influences like tariffs and weather to guide strategic network adjustments and mitigate potential risks. This data-centric approach translates to cost savings, increased efficiency, and a more resilient supply chain.

Epicor

Leveraging Microsoft Azure's AI capabilities, Epicor enhances its business solutions for distributors and manufacturers. They focus on optimizing supply chain management and logistics while exploring integrations with Microsoft's speech-to-text and advanced search technology to further improve the user experience. This commitment to AI innovation promises more streamlined operations and intuitive user interactions.

Echo Global Logistics

Echo, a transportation startup, embraces AI to simplify shipping for its customers. Their AI-powered platform provides swift, secure, and cost-effective logistics solutions. From rate negotiations and procurement to shipment tracking and carrier management, Echo offers a comprehensive suite of services, empowering businesses with greater control and transparency over their logistics operations.

Infor

Infor's intelligent logistics solutions bring together cutting-edge algorithms, optimization tools, and ML to bridge the gap between the virtual and physical worlds. This data-driven approach empowers businesses to gain valuable insights and make informed decisions across various aspects of their logistics network, including planning, procurement, financing, supply management, visibility, transportation, and warehouse management. By embracing AI, Infor empowers businesses with an intelligent and interconnected logistics ecosystem.

Amazon Web Services

As one of the pioneers in adopting AI, Amazon has long been benefiting from the efficiency brought by this technology. Amazon utilizes AI to predict customer demand, optimize warehouse operations, and enhance last-mile delivery efficiency. Amazon Web Services (AWS) assist in route optimization, ensuring that drivers use real-time data to navigate the best routes and avoid traffic and any possible delays. This ensures that customers get their orders delivered on time and in great condition. For perishable goods, timely delivery is a must; therefore, AI integration ensures Amazon grocers maintain product quality and freshness. This might even be the reason behind Amazon's e-commerce dominance.

Walmart

By harnessing AI algorithms, Walmart can analyze vast sets of historical and real-time data to predict consumer demand with remarkable accuracy. This capability enables the retail giant to optimize its inventory levels, ensuring that products are available when and where customers need them. Furthermore, AI-driven route optimization enhances the efficiency of Walmart's logistics, minimizing transportation costs and ensuring timely deliveries. This strategic implementation of AI not only leads to substantial cost savings for Walmart but also translates into improved customer service, as products are more readily available, contributing to a seamless and satisfying shopping experience.

Maersk

In the realm of competitive transportation rates, the Maersk chatbot automatically secures a quote, saving the company from lengthy negotiations. Maersk's AI also automates much of the documentation process, reducing errors, speeding up customs clearance, and making the entire shipping process smoother and faster for both Maersk and its customers. It showcases how AI can streamline even mundane tasks, saving time and resources. This chatbot not only secures competitive rates but also acts as a personalized assistant for customers, answering questions, tracking shipments, and even suggesting optimal shipping options. Maersk's commitment to AI shows us the future of logistics. A future where intelligent systems optimize every aspect of the shipping process, from route planning to warehouse operations. This makes global trade more efficient, sustainable, and accessible than ever before.

Unilever

Unilever, a global consumer goods company, has strategically employed AI tools to identify and engage with diverse suppliers worldwide. This proactive approach not only proves invaluable during supply disruptions by providing alternative sourcing options but also aligns with Unilever's commitment to fostering supply-base diversification. Through AI-driven supplier discovery, Unilever enhances its resilience in the face of challenges, ensuring a stable and diverse supply chain. Moreover, this initiative creates opportunities for smaller to medium-sized businesses, offering them a chance to collaborate with a corporate giant like Unilever. By leveraging AI, Unilever not only fortifies its own supply network but also contributes to the growth and global market access of smaller enterprises, fostering a more inclusive and robust business ecosystem.

Siemens

Siemens began searching for ways to obtain substitute suppliers when they encountered a scarcity of Suryln, a specialized resin that is utilized in medical product packaging. It even located more than 150 distributors of this patented product using the AI-powered Scoutbee. Scoutbee also quickly arranged the import and shipping documents for Suryln from international distributors. If this was done manually, it could have taken several weeks to months, yet AI solved this supply shock within a few days. Even Siemens director of supply chain, Michael Klinger, admitted that while technology does not prevent supply shocks or even warn them before they happen, it provides reliable information that aids faster relief than any human can provide (Van Hoek & Lacity, 2023).

Coyote Logistics

Using predictive analytics and ML, among several other technologies, Coyote Logistics matches the customers shipping information with external data, like weather and traffic. This helps shippers predict and manage real-time supply chain issues before they arise. Shippers can then arrange for alternative shipping to ensure that customers still receive their products on schedule.

GE Aviation

Like Boeing, GE Aviation uses AI to predict engine failures, allowing airlines to schedule preventative maintenance and avoid delays. AI monitors sensor data from equipment and vehicles to predict potential failures before they occur, preventing costly breakdowns and production disruptions.

BENEFITS AND CHALLENGES OF USING AI IN SUPPLY CHAIN MANAGEMENT

Leveraging various AI technologies, AI in supply chain management holds the promise of optimizing processes, enhancing efficiency, and fortifying decision-making. The capacity to analyze vast datasets in real-time allows for improved demand forecasting, inventory optimization, and logistics planning. However, alongside these advantages, challenges emerge, encompassing aspects such as initial implementation costs, the need for specialized technical expertise, and potential job displacement. Striking a delicate balance between maximizing the benefits and mitigating challenges becomes paramount as businesses navigate the dynamic landscape of AI-infused supply chain management.

Benefits

Improved Forecasting and Demand Planning

As seen with pioneering companies using AI, it helps businesses make better predictions about future demand and optimize their inventory levels. By analyzing big data, past trends, and current market conditions, AI can more accurately predict when things will run out or be too plentiful. This means companies can keep just the right amount of stuff on hand without wasting money or losing sales due to stockouts.

Optimized Inventory Management

Using AI algorithms, businesses can manage their inventories more efficiently by finding the sweet spot between keeping enough supplies on hand and avoiding unnecessary expenses associated with storing extra items. With optimized inventory levels, companies save money on storage space and minimize the chance of disappointed customers because products are always available when they need them.

Enhanced Logistics and Route Optimization

AI can also help plan the most efficient routes for deliveries and reduce fuel consumption and carbon emissions. By considering factors like traffic, weather, and delivery time windows, AI can find the best way to get packages where they need to go without wasting time or resources.

Predictive Maintenance for Equipment

Combining predictive analytics, ML, and CV, AI algorithms can predict when it is time to fix equipment before it breaks down, saving time and money by catching problems early. This also helps extend the life of machinery and equipment, so they last longer and do not have to be replaced as often.

Real-Time Visibility and Tracking

With AI, businesses can track their shipments in real-time, giving them greater insight into their supply chains. This makes it easier to identify potential issues and solve problems quickly, ensuring that goods arrive on time and in good condition.

Enhanced Supplier Relationship Management

Finally, AI can analyze how well suppliers are doing and look for ways to work together more effectively. By understanding which suppliers are reliable and which ones might cause problems, businesses can build stronger partnerships and avoid delays or shortages caused by poorly performing vendors.

Challenges

Data Security

Imagine entrusting your precious family recipes to a digital cookbook, but fearing malicious hackers could replace them with inedible concoctions. That is the concern with data security in AI-powered supply chains. Sensitive data like shipping routes, supplier details, and inventory levels are invaluable targets for cyberattacks. A malicious competitor can manipulate shipment data to disrupt deliveries, causing delays and lost profits. Robust cybersecurity measures like encryption, access controls, and regular vulnerability assessments are critical to preserving the integrity and competitiveness of your supply chain.

Scaling the System

Scaling AI systems for growing operations requires proactive planning. Imagine adding new warehouses across the country, each relying on AI for logistics. You need a system that can seamlessly integrate data from all locations, adjust algorithms for diverse inventory flows, and optimize routes across a wider network. Investing in modular, scalable AI solutions that can adapt to your expanding needs is essential.

Infrastructure Costs

AI solutions may require additional hardware or internet upgrades to handle complex data processing. You cannot afford to have less-than-average equipment or shaky tracking devices while transporting sensitive cargo. Investing in robust internet infrastructure and potentially new hardware, like delivery drones, might be necessary, but consider it an investment in the efficiency and accuracy of your AI-powered supply chain.

Training Employees

Think of introducing AI as welcoming a friendly robot assistant into your warehouse. It can lift heavy boxes, but will your team know how to operate its controls and optimize its work? Employee training is crucial for successful AI integration. Untrained staff could confuse commands, leading the robot to stack boxes precariously or block crucial pathways. Therefore, you must invest in comprehensive training programs to equip your team with the skills and knowledge needed to work effectively with AI, maximizing its benefits and minimizing disruption.

Operating Costs

Owning an AI-powered supply chain is like having a self-driving delivery truck; it might be convenient, but it needs regular maintenance and occasional software updates. Ongoing operating costs are an important consideration. Imagine your self-driving truck getting lost due to outdated navigation software. Regular system updates, maintenance to ensure smooth operation, and troubleshooting potential issues all contribute to the ongoing costs of AI. However, consider these costs as an investment in the ongoing optimization and reliability of your supply chain, improving efficiency and potentially offsetting them through cost savings in other areas.

A business that has a grip on supply chain management is bound to have satisfied customers and consistently lock in profits with timely deliveries and order fulfillment. Leveraging AI, organizations are able to forecast demand, manage inventories, plan transportation, and automate logistics. This chapter closes the selected examples of areas where AI is making strides in business it is implemented in. The last chapter of the book provides an overview of the future trends and predictions of this digital space.

10

FUTURE TRENDS AND PREDICTIONS OF ARTIFICIAL INTELLIGENCE IN BUSINESS

With its current value of over $200 billion, the AI market is expected to balloon to nearly $2 trillion by 2030, representing a more than tenfold increase (Thormundsson, 2023). This indicates the staggering mass adoption of this evolutionary technology. In this last chapter, we will study the anticipated AI future, starting with the imminent trends and advancements and how they will impact businesses. We will also look at the continuous limiting factors responsible for the current integration pace as well as dive into the remedies to prepare for the future. We will close it with mind-blowing predictions experts anticipate about AI.

EMERGING TRENDS AND ADVANCEMENTS IN AI FOR BUSINESS APPLICATIONS

As AI continues to evolve, its impact on business is becoming profound, reshaping industries, creating new opportunities, and challenging us to reimagine how we work and live. This section succinctly discusses upcoming AI developments and how they are bound to impact business applications.

Development of Powerful AI Hardware and Software

Imagine a computer that can solve problems in minutes that would take traditional machines years. That is the promise of quantum computing, a revolutionary hardware advancement pioneered by companies like IBM and Google. With the ability to handle vast amounts of data and perform complex calculations simultaneously, quantum computers will equip AI systems with unparalleled capabilities. This will enable them to tackle intricate tasks in fields like drug discovery, materials science, and financial modeling with unprecedented speed and accuracy.

Increasing Availability of Large Datasets for AI Training

The digital age has unleashed a torrent of data, flowing from our online activities, social media interactions, and the ubiquitous Internet of Things (IoT). This abundance of data acts as the lifeblood of AI, providing the raw material for training its algorithms. By analyzing vast datasets, AI systems refine their learning processes, leading to improved performance in diverse fields. For example, in healthcare, AI analyzes patient records from millions of individuals, identifying patterns and correlations that would be impossible for human clinicians to decipher. This leads to more accurate diagnoses, personalized treatment recommendations, and ultimately improved patient outcomes.

Development of New AI Algorithms and Techniques

We have established that AI is not just about crunching complex numbers and processing vast amounts of data; it is also about getting creative. Advancements in algorithms, like Generative Adversarial Networks (GANs), are pushing the boundaries of AI's creative capabilities. GANs, pioneered by Ian Goodfellow, pit two neural networks against each other: one generates data while the other tries to distinguish it from real data. This training process produces stunningly realistic images, videos, and even music. Imagine marketing campaigns with hyper-personalized visuals or immersive virtual reality experiences, all crafted by AI.

As evidenced by the tools I shared in Chapter 3, the development of new AI algorithms and techniques is not only a futuristic concept but already happening. AI can already generate realistic simulations of complex phenomena, allowing scientists to test hypotheses and develop new theories without the limitations of real-world experiments. The possibilities for AI-powered creativity are endless, from revolutionizing the entertainment industry to creating personalized art and design experiences.

Integration of AI With Other Technologies (IoT and Blockchain)

AI's potential is further amplified when it joins forces with other cutting-edge technologies. The IoT, a network of interconnected devices, generates real-time data that AI can analyze and act upon instantaneously. This dynamic duo is transforming industries like smart cities, where AI crunches data from traffic sensors to optimize traffic flow and energy consumption, leading to smoother commutes and a more sustainable urban environment.

The fusion of AI with blockchain, a decentralized and tamper-proof ledger technology, introduces another layer of security and transparency. By combining AI's analytical prowess with blockchain's secure record-keeping capabilities, we can envision secure and traceable transactions in supply chain management, financial services, and beyond.

ADDRESSING POTENTIAL CHALLENGES AND PREPARING FOR THE FUTURE

Although we discussed industry-specific challenges in previous chapters, I believe we must, once again, bring home the limitations in this chapter. The focus here is to reflect on the continuous challenges that may slow down AI adoption and how businesses can prepare for the future. Addressing futuristic challenges is a wise move to remain informed so as to keep up with this fast-paced technology.

Continuous AI Challenges That Affect the Future

The Price Tag of Progress

As seen in earlier chapters on implementing AI in different disciplines, the main challenge is that developing and deploying cutting-edge AI solutions comes at a premium. With emerging AI tools proving to be more efficient, the price tag of implementing this technology in business might continue to increase. This can exacerbate existing digital divides and limit access to powerful technologies for smaller businesses. This will also continue to increase the existing wealth gap between established companies and those struggling to find their footing.

The AI Talent Gap

Considering the technological demands of the most anticipated and hypothetical AI types, general AI and superintelligence, most people are not skilled enough to comprehend and manage what is imminent. As AI applications grow in complexity, the demand for skilled professionals will continue to skyrocket. This gap in expertise can hinder widespread adoption and hamper innovation.

Experts Do Not Understand Why AI Hallucinations Happen

Even though experts agree that AI has its limitations, there has not been any progress since that realization. If AI models continue to be delusional and make stuff up, this will exacerbate the lack of trust in the technology with so much potential to improve our lives. This will delay the rate of mass adoption and possibly hinder its progress.

Hindrance of Human Resources Growth

As more and more tasks are automated, there is a high risk of most human resources becoming obsolete. While there is also a growing potential for teams to be exposed to more AI-related skills, most organizations will lose skills that are meant for people's intellectual growth. This is a threat to society's well-being and the pursuit of roles they find fulfillment in.

Continuous Ethical Conundrums

Although early adopters are working tirelessly to make this space safe, the ethical implications of AI, from bias and privacy concerns to potential job displacement, continue to demand careful consideration. The current lack of clear guidelines and regulations still poses significant risks. Unless the regulatory bodies advance at an exponential rate, they will not catch up with the advancement of AI. This is an ongoing challenge because, by the time they find a solution to the current ethical concerns, there is a high possibility that new challenges will arise as regulations lag behind.

Preparing for the Future

Investing in AI Research and Development

Increased support for AI research and development, similar to Silicon Valley's venture capitalist initiatives, can democratize access and accelerate AI advancement for all. Therefore, governments and companies should invest more in AI research and development to make it more accessible and affordable for everyone.

Sharing Knowledge and Resources

By sharing what we know and making AI tools more accessible, we can lower the barriers to entry for smaller players and help them use AI effectively. Organizations must start equipping their existing workforce with relevant AI skills through training programs and educational initiatives. Encouraging STEM education, promoting inclusion in tech fields, and attracting global AI talent can also address the demand more effectively.

Developing Robust Ethical Frameworks

There must be robust ethical frameworks in place. AI is not an American or any nation's concern, but a global one. Therefore, establishing international collaboration and industry-wide standards for responsible AI development, deployment, and usage is essential. Moreover, governments and regulatory bodies must increase their learning speed in order to catch up. Alternatively, regulatory bodies must come from the group of AI innovators and early adopters, as they are the ones who understand the space better and are in a privileged position to make ethical decisions about the use of AI.

Proactive Dialogue and Public Engagement

People must stop tiptoeing around AI and being skeptical without any in-depth knowledge. Because, whether they avoid this technology like a plague or embrace it, they cannot stop its advancement. In fact, most people are already oblivious victims of AI, where it is impacting their lives without even knowing it. Considering how giant companies are already using data to access and serve customers, we are already living in the AI era. They might as well be informed so that they can make wise decisions regarding their level of involvement. Open discussions about AI's potential benefits and risks, involving diverse stakeholders, can mitigate public fears and foster collective responsibility.

BUSINESS-RELATED PREDICTIONS OF AI

Research indicates that the AI market in healthcare will be worth $187 billion by 2030, a staggering improvement from its $11 billion market in 2021 (Stewart, 2023). Such an astronomical rise in a sensitive industry could only mean that AI would have proved its competence and been deemed worthy of handling more responsibilities. If medical doctors trust the capabilities of AI with matters of life and death, how much more can it do in businesses and other sectors? Although directly and indirectly related to businesses, this section discusses several predictions about AI and how it will further impact our lives and work in the future.

More Opportunities for Human-AI Collaboration

As AI evolves, collaboration between humans and AI entities will intensify, creating synergistic partnerships. This will lead to enhanced productivity and creativity as AI augments human capabilities, leading to innovative solutions and improved decision-making.

Advancements in Data Security

Continuous technological progress will fortify data security measures, ensuring robust protection against cyber threats. This will lead to heightened confidence in utilizing AI for sensitive tasks, fostering increased adoption across industries with a strengthened security infrastructure.

AI Will Reach Human-Level Intelligence

Although there are controversies about the hypothetical AGI and artificial superintelligence, particularly about when these advanced AI levels will be effective, there is no denying the fact that this technology is advancing at an alarming and exponential rate. While it might take decades for the AI singularity to be achieved, some experts predict that AI systems will match human intelligence in the next 10 years. Current AI systems are limited by data and computational power; therefore, reaching human-level intelligence will be determined by advancements in quantum computing. Imagine having systems that match the problem-solving, decision-making, and creativity abilities of human business managers. With AI handling complex cognitive tasks and transforming industries and workflows, this will mean accelerated automation and efficiency in business.

AI Will Enhance Human Intelligence

AI will act as a cognitive aid, supplementing human intelligence and facilitating more informed decision-making. Tables are turning; humans taught machines how to think and reason by feeding them enormous amounts of data. Now, it is expected that humans will learn from the findings of AI if they do not want to remain behind as the technology advances. AI contributing complementary insights to human expertise will have a huge impact on business, improving problem-solving, strategic planning, and creativity.

A Rise of Human Cyborgs

There are people currently suffering from autoimmune diseases that limit their mobility and other bodily functionalities. The idea of becoming a cyborg may sound ludicrous to people who have full vitality, but exploring the idea of having artificial limbs and other parts that enhance human life is not far-fetched. If there is a slight chance that integration of AI with human bodies will enhance physical and cognitive capabilities, there is definitely bound to be a rise in human cyborgs. While this sounds like an expensive surgery, I believe there will be people and organizations funding this mission to preserve human life. Now, how will this affect businesses? I hear you ask. Think of how many people have been out of jobs because of physical and mental impairments. Imagine having creative people in organizations remain and being given the opportunity to remain in their positions. No business would have to suffer losses from their key human resources. Therefore, potential advancements in healthcare, performance optimization, and human-machine interfaces lead to novel business opportunities.

Content Creation Will Be Tailored to AI Capabilities

Content creation tools are already adapting to AI capabilities, generating personalized and contextually relevant content. This is expected to continue rising and reach new heights. Instead of mopping about how AI is replacing human talent, adaptive artists and content creators are also incorporating AI into their craft. This allows them to grow with this technology and reach the masses. The same applies to businesses that are ready to collaborate with AI. They are bound to reach enhanced marketing strategies, customer engagement, and communication as AI-driven content aligns with target audience preferences.

Self-Driving Cars Will Dominate the Roads Worldwide

Like any controversial technology that was initially resisted, autonomous vehicle technology will mature, leading to widespread adoption and dominance on the roads. While this will cause disruption in the transportation and supply chain industries, it will also increase safety and efficiency in logistics. The rise in self-driving cars will also free people's time, allowing them to work from anywhere. You could be engaging in a business conference call while on the way without getting a fine or paying a human chauffer. This could potentially shorten a workday and allow people to focus on other income-generating roles.

AI Will Create New Job Opportunities

According to 2022 predictions, approximately 2.3 million new jobs will be created, while 1.8 million existing jobs will be eliminated, due to the advancement of AI (Thormundsson, 2022). While AI is replacing some jobs, it is also creating new roles requiring human skills. This trend is expected to continue, as there is a need to monitor AI systems and verify that there are no inconsistencies with AI-driven decisions. I already mentioned that there is a fear of careers that people are passionate about becoming obsolete. This can be seen with the rise in science and technology-based careers, as they are more inclined toward AI. This kills a dynamic job landscape and career diversity. It might lead to the elimination of some businesses as more people ditch their careers in fear of AI replacing them. Nobody knows the future; therefore, things might work out differently.

Enactment of Ethical Rules and Regulations for AI

Societal awareness ensures that businesses integrate ethical considerations into every stage of AI development and deployment. This means prioritizing human well-being, privacy, and security over efficiency or profit alone. It means using AI to empower individuals, not control them. Increasing societal awareness will drive the establishment of comprehensive ethical guidelines and regulations for AI. This will improve accountability, transparency, and responsible AI practices, ensuring ethical use and mitigating risks in business applications. Remember, increasing societal awareness is not a passive process. It requires active engagement from individuals, communities, and institutions. By raising our voices, advocating for responsible AI practices, and pushing for robust ethical frameworks, we can ensure that AI becomes a force for good, a tool that lifts humanity to new heights while safeguarding our values and securing a brighter future for all.

Congratulations on reading until this point. As you have noticed throughout this book, AI is advancing at an alarming rate, regardless of whether some people are skeptical about embracing it or not. It is possible that some of these trending and upcoming advancements will become obsolete or replaced by new ones in no time. However, they pave the way for the future and keep us in the loop so that we are not far behind. You can read through the key takeaways recapped in the following conclusion.

WHAT YOU CAN DO NOW

With AI in your toolkit, you're ready to accelerate your business, and that puts you in the perfect position to spread the word.

Simply by sharing your honest opinion of this book and a little about your own experience with AI, you'll help new readers sift through the noise and find the information their business needs.

Thank you so much for your support. I truly appreciate it.

CONCLUSION

Embracing AI in a responsible and strategic manner can significantly contribute to business success in the rapidly evolving digital landscape. Behemoth companies at the forefront of technological advancement are a perfect example of how leveraging AI is a great move for any organization. I get that you may not have had similar advantages and resources to be an early AI adopter. However, I hope that reading this book and witnessing the real-world examples of tech giants like Amazon and Netflix has given you a new perspective and inspiration to test the waters yourself. Being engaged until this point is a great sign that you finish what you start—an impressive business ethic. It also delights me to know that you invested in more knowledge about this digital space, while others choose to reject AI without even considering basic knowledge at the very least.

To recap, I introduced the AI concept as the simulation of human intelligence in machines and computer systems. When exploring the ability of machines to think, learn, understand, and reason like humans, AI pioneers also discovered the possibility of AI to not only emulate human cognitive abilities but also how this enables machines to improve our lives. From solving complex problems to absorbing and processing chunks of data in a fraction of a second without getting exhausted, these are some of the great AI abilities that can bring efficiency to any industry in which it is deployed.

Chapter 2 highlighted the common types of AI, starting with the current narrow AI, which is fairly easy to deploy as it focuses on specific tasks. Narrow AI has its own limitations, such as... As such, innovators are exploring possibilities around general AI, which is believed to match human intelligence. While it may seem farfetched due to its difficulty to develop with the current limited resources, some experts anticipate that general AI is closer than we think and that it will revolutionize industries in a massive way. Lastly, there is the hypothetical artificial superintelligence, which is expected to surpass human intelligence. Arguably, this technology is potentially becoming a threat to humanity as people fear that humans will not be able to control it, adding to the fictionalized AI takeover. Perhaps this is the reason most people are skeptical about exploring the possibilities that AI brings.

However, the interesting top trending tools discussed in Chapter 3 indicate how AI is transforming the way we work and collaborate with AI to enhance productivity and maximize resources. Popular tools like ChatGPT, DALL-E 3, and

MidJourney have beginner-friendly interfaces, enabling anyone to explore with AI. Various tools combine ML, NLP, and CV to assist users in managing their projects, creating content, and streamlining workflows. Besides lack of knowledge and the feared "AI takeover," another major setback delaying mass adoption is the issue of ethics. Current AI systems pose a threat to data security, perpetuate bias and unfairness, lack explainability, and threaten job security. Addressing these issues should be everyone's concern, particularly industry leaders and governments. Organizations using AI must be accountable and responsible enough to educate their teams, advocate for open-source AI tools, ensure transparency, and train their systems with diverse data.

Chapter 5 took a deeper dive into the main topic of the book, focusing on the implementation of AI in business processes. It addressed easy-to-follow steps to integrate AI into existing teams to avoid overwhelming organizations with knowledge and financial burdens. Gradually integrating AI into any business overcomes cost, complexity, and ethical challenges while ensuring that best practices are adhered to. Successive chapters shed more light on how specific businesses leverage AI in their operations. With AI in CRM, organizations can leverage chatbots to service their clients. AI in data analytics demonstrated how AI uses predictive analysis to study data and automatically create comprehensive reports in half the time it would take human data analysts. AI in supply chain, marketing, and sales demonstrates how organizations optimize resources like time and money because businesses target customers who already have the intention to buy, know what products to stock, and ensure customer satisfaction by delivering demanded products on time. I also shared the challenges that these industries face due to the limitations of AI.

The last chapter brought home the idea that AI is in constant motion, exponentially evolving. Therefore, it is crucial that we all stay engaged and alert toward its advancements so that nothing catches us by surprise. AI future trends and predictions require us to be more knowledgeable, as experts anticipate that this digital space will continue transforming lives and businesses in a phenomenal way. In a nutshell, *Artificial Intelligence for Business* is a comprehensive guide covering AI basics, benefits, and challenges involved so that business leaders can have an understanding of its potential and pitfalls before implementing it in their respective fields. I hope you found it useful and practical to take your next step in exploring AI. Remember that this book is slightly advanced from the first title, *Artificial Intelligence Pushing Boundaries: Is It Worth It?*, which I recommend for anyone looking for a beginner-friendly introduction to AI.

I've also conveniently included a glossary that explains a list of terms you encountered in this book on the next page. As you learn deeper about AI and possibly get firsthand experience by implementing it into your business, I wish you all the success in your journey. I would greatly appreciate you leaving a review on Amazon so that others can easily find this book and also start their journey with enough knowledge of this evolutionary technology.

GLOSSARY

AlphaGo: An AI program developed by DeepMind to play the board game Go.

Ameca: A humanoid robot developed by Hanson Robotics.

Anomaly Detection: Identifying unusual patterns in data to detect fraud, errors, or system failures.

Artificial Intelligence: The simulation of human intelligence processes, such as the ability to think, learn, understand, and reason, by machines or computer systems.

Artificial Super-Intelligence: A hypothetical AI that surpasses human intelligence.

Big Data: The massive volume of structured and unstructured data that businesses deal with.

Black Box: Refers to an AI system whose internal workings are not transparent or easily understandable.

Blind Spots: Areas or aspects of AI models or systems that are not well understood or inadequately addressed.

Blockchain: A distributed ledger technology that ensures secure and transparent data sharing.

Blockchain-Based AI: Combining AI with blockchain technology for secure and transparent data sharing.

Business Intelligence (BI) Tools: AI-infused platforms offering intelligent insights and recommendations.

Chatbots: AI-driven programs designed to simulate conversations with human users.

Cloud Computing: Providing computing services over the internet, making AI more accessible.

Computer Vision: A field of AI that enables machines to interpret and make decisions based on visual data from the world, such as images and videos.

Customer Churn: The rate at which customers stop doing business with a company; often analyzed using AI for predictive purposes.

Cyborg: A being with both organic and bio-mechatronic body parts; in the context of AI, it may refer to humans with integrated AI enhancements.

Data Governance: Implementing practices to ensure data quality, security, and compliance.

Deep Learning: A subset of ML that involves neural networks with multiple layers, enabling the processing of complex data.

Differential Privacy: Adds carefully calibrated noise to data, ensuring statistical accuracy while protecting individual privacy.

Edge AI: Processing data at the source rather than in the cloud for real-time insights.

Ethics: The principles and guidelines addressing the moral implications and responsible use of AI.

Expert Systems: Early AI systems designed to mimic human expertise in specific domains (e.g. DENDRAL, MYCIN, XCON).

Federated Learning: A privacy-preserving ML technique where training data remains decentralized on devices.

General AI: A theoretical AI that can perform any intellectual task that a human can.

Generative AI: Creating new content like images, music, and text.

Hallucinations: Refers to incorrect or false outputs generated by an AI model.

Homomorphic Encryption: A technique that allows computations on encrypted data, enabling analysis without decryption.

Humanoid: A robot designed to resemble and imitate human behavior.

Image Pilot (Hivemind): An AI pilot developed by Shield AI capable of flying various aircraft.

Internet of Things (IoT): The network of interconnected devices that communicate and share data.

Machine Learning: A type of AI that allows computers to learn from data and make decisions without explicit programming.

Narrow AI: AI designed for specific tasks or domains, such as playing chess or driving a car.

Natural Language Processing: AI that analyzes and understands human language.

Predictive Analysis: Using AI to make informed predictions about future trends and behaviors.

Robotic Process Automation (RPA): The use of software robots to automate repetitive tasks.

Sentiment Analysis: Analyzing text to gauge the emotional tone and opinion.

Sophia: A humanoid robot developed by Hanson Robotics.

Speech Recognition: Converting spoken language into text.

Synthetic Data Generation: Artificially generated data created to mimic real data characteristics.

Virtual Assistants: AI-driven tools that assist users with tasks using natural language.

REFERENCES

AI Andy. (2023, November 12). *6 best AI tools for business [effortless business productivity].* [Video]. YouTube. https://www.youtube.com/watch?v=oUH0Cf5y4H8

AI in sales and marketing: Transforming teams and reshaping hiring. (2023, August 30). Morgan Mckinley. https://www.morganmckinley.com/article/ai-in-sales-marketing-transforming-teams-and-reshaping-hiring

AI Uncovered. (2023a, August 24). *The 15 best AI tools for business (so far)* [Video]. YouTube. https://www.youtube.com/watch?v=rudddwkpotE

AI Uncovered. (2023b, November 14). *The 10 shocking AI predictions for the next 10 years* [Video]. YouTube. https://www.youtube.com/watch?v=R016p45QT5w

Aslam, M. (2023, April 25). *8 steps to successfully implement AI in your business.* LinkedIn. https://www.linkedin.com/pulse/8-steps-successfully-implement-ai-your-business-misbahul-aslam

Baker, V. E., & O'Connor, D. E. (1989). Expert systems for configuration at Digital: XCON and beyond. *Communications of the ACM, 32*(3), 298+. Gale Academic Onefile. https://go.gale.com/ps/i.do?id=GALE%7CA7100854&sid=googleScholar&v=2.1&it=r&linkaccess=abs&issn=00010782&p=AONE&sw=w&userGroupName=anon%7Eab9542bd&aty=open-web-entry

Basello, J., & Feeley, S. (2021, August 25). *The history of AI in manufacturing.* Blog.radwell.com. https://blog.radwell.com/the-history-of-ai-in-manufacturing

Bjerregaard, L. (2023, May 26). *GE, Waygate partner on AI-powered engine inspections.* Aviation Week Network. https://aviationweek.com/mro/emerging-technologies/ge-waygate-partner-ai-powered-engine-inspections

Blanco, S. (2023, June 13). *Report: Tesla Autopilot involved in 736 crashes since 2019.* Car and Driver. https://www.caranddriver.com/news/a44185487/report-tesla-autopilot-crashes-since-2019/

Bowman, J. (2023, November 13). *10 top companies using AI in a compelling way.* The Motley Fool. https://www.fool.com/investing/stock-market/market-sectors/information-technology/ai-stocks/companies-that-use-ai/

Business Solution. (2023, May 27). *5 best AI CRM software systems to 10X your customer relationship management in 2023* [Video]. YouTube. https://www.youtube.com/watch?v=Ln-MDHW4WB0

Caballero, B. (2023, July 10). *How to use Zoho CRM in 7 easy steps.* Fit Small Business. https://fitsmallbusiness.com/how-to-use-zoho/

Carlow University. (2022, February 21). *How artificial intelligence is shaping data analytics.* https://blog.carlow.edu/2022/02/21/how-artificial-intelligence-is-shaping-data-analytics/

Carpena, M. (2023, October 27). *The advantages and disadvantages of using AI in marketing.* WebFX. https://www.webfx.com/blog/marketing/ai-marketing-advantages-disadvantages/

Chambers, C. (2023, July). *Happy 43rd anniversary to the real-world application of AI!* LinkedIn. https://www.linkedin.com/posts/chrischambers1784_innovation-team-work-activity-7081278914798448640-KQ9O

Champion, A. (2023, September 28). *AI in supply chain management: Use cases, impact, & more.* Flowspace. https://flow.space/blog/ai-in-supply-chain/

Chia, A. (2023, October). *5 unique ways to use AI in data analytics.* DataCamp. https://www.datacamp.com/blog/unique-ways-to-use-ai-in-data-analytics

Dangut, M. D., Jennions, I. K., King, S., & Skaf, Z. (2022). A rare failure detection model for aircraft predictive maintenance using a deep hybrid learning approach. *Neural Computing and Applications, 35.* https://doi.org/10.1007/s00521-022-07167-8

Deveau, R., Griffin, S. J., & Reis, S. (2023). *Marketing and sales soar with generative AI.* McKinsey. https://www.mckinsey.com/capabilities/growth-marketing-and-sales/our-insights/ai-powered-marketing-and-sales-reach-new-heights-with-generative-ai

Drury, K. (2023, May 10). *Is Amazon's AI-powered supply chain the secret to its dominance?* The Motley Fool. https://www.fool.com/investing/2023/05/10/is-amazons-ai-powered-supply-chain-the-secret-to-i/

Duggal, N. (2023, November 24). *Top 10 artificial intelligence technologies in 2024.* Simplilearn. https://www.simplilearn.com/top-artificial-intelligence-technologies-article

Five AI technologies that you need to know. (n.d.). Sas. https://www.sas.com/en_za/insights/articles/analytics/five-ai-technologies.html

Frankenfield, J. (2023, December 4). *Artificial intelligence: What it is and how it is used.* Investopedia. https://www.investopedia.com/terms/a/artificial-intelligence-ai.asp

Gadzhi, I. (2023, August 15). *These 7 AI tools will make you rich* [Video]. YouTube. https://www.youtube.com/watch?v=-qReeg7imGc

Gail, E. (2023, September 12). *How artificial intelligence can impact supply chains and logistics.* Cointelegraph. https://cointelegraph.com/explained/how-artifi cial-intelligence-can-impact-supply-chains-and-logistics

General Assembly. (2023, September 7). *Beyond tomorrow: 5 ways business leaders can prepare for the future of AI.* General Assembly Blog. https://gener alassemb.ly/blog/beyond-tomorrow-5-ways-business-leaders-can-prepare-for-the-future-of-ai/

Google DeepMind. (2020). *AlphaGo - the movie | full documentary* [Video]. YouTube. https://www.youtube.com/watch?v=WXuK6gekU1Y

Goutham, R. (2021, March 24). *A beginner's guide to understanding the buzz words - AI, ML, NLP, deep learning, computer vision....* The Startup. https://medium. com/swlh/a-beginners-guide-to-understanding-the-buzz-words-ai-ml-nlp-deep-learning-computer-vision-a877ee1c2cde

Great Learning Team. (2023, December 11). *10 hottest artificial intelligence (AI) technologies in 2024 that are changing the game.* Great Learning. https://www. mygreatlearning.com/blog/artificial-intelligence-technologies/

Gulati, A. (2023, November 20). *AI in supply chain: Challenges, benefits & implementation.* Knowledge Hut. https://www.knowledgehut.com/blog/data-science/ai-in-supply-chain

Howarth, J. (2023, November 29). *57 new AI statistics (Dec 2023).* Exploding Topics. https://explodingtopics.com/blog/ai-statistics

HubSpot: Inbound marketing, sales, and service software. (2023). HubSpot. https:// www.hubspot.com/

IBM Newsroom. (2023, December 5). *AI alliance launches as an international community of leading technology developers, researchers, and adopters collaborating together to advance open, safe, responsible AI.* IBM. https://newsroom.ibm. com/AI-Alliance-Launches-as-an-International-Community-of-Leading-Technology-Developers,-Researchers,-and-Adopters-Collaborating-Together-to-Advance-Open,-Safe,-Responsible-AI

Intellipaat. (2023, February 24). *Top 10 ChatGPT alternatives to use in 2023 | ChatGPT alternative | Intellipaat* [Video]. YouTube. https://www.youtube. com/watch?v=mT-SD_Tz7rw

Jankoski, B. B. (2023). *Artificial intelligence pushing boundaries, is it worth it?* Pef Thirteen, LLC. My Book

Jasminara, S. (2023a, May 8). *Historical evolution of AI in marketing.* LinkedIn.

https://www.linkedin.com/pulse/historical-evolution-ai-marketing-syed-jasminara

Jasminara, S. (2023b, June 13). *Benefits and challenges of AI in marketing.* LinkedIn. https://www.linkedin.com/pulse/benefits-challenges-ai-marketing-syed-jasminara

Kurey, B. (2023, September 21). *Finding the right starting point for AI in sales.* SBI. https://sbigrowth.com/insights/finding-the-right-starting-point-for-ai-in-sales

Learn With Shopify. (2023). *10 AI tools to run your business from A to Z* [Video]. YouTube. https://www.youtube.com/watch?v=BYpJQ0pYBVE

Leonard-Barton, D., & Sviokla, J. J. (1988, March). *Putting expert systems to work.* Harvard Business Review. https://hbr.org/1988/03/putting-expert-systems-to-work

Marr, B. (2021, July 2). *The 10 best examples of how companies use artificial intelligence in practice.* Bernard Marr. https://bernardmarr.com/the-10-best-examples-of-how-companies-use-artificial-intelligence-in-practice/

Marvin, R., & Horowitz, B. (2018, November 12). *10 steps to adopting artificial intelligence in your business.* PCMAG. https://www.pcmag.com/news/10-steps-to-adopting-artificial-intelligence-in-your-business

Mattison, R. (2023, September 19). *10 best AI tools for business efficiency in 2023.* ThoughtSpot. https://www.thoughtspot.com/data-trends/ai/best-ai-tools-for-business

McCallum, S. (2023, July 10). Threads app signs up 100m users in less than a week. *BBC News.* https://www.bbc.com/news/technology-66153244

McFarland, A. (2023, December 1). *13 best AI tools for business (December 2023).* Unite.AI. https://www.unite.ai/best-ai-tools-for-business/

Mercedes-Benz USA reports Q1 2023 total sales of 75,701 vehicles. (2023, April 12). MBUSA Newsroom. https://media.mbusa.com/releases/release-0cbff62111a361ef6df50814ca13c257-mercedes-benz-usa-reports-q1-2023-total-sales-of-75701-vehicles

Mulli, J. (2023, October 31). *AI vs data analysts: Top 6 limitations impacting the future of analytics.* KDnuggets. https://www.kdnuggets.com/ai-vs-data-analysts-top-6-limitations-impacting-the-future-of-analytics

Newsroom. (2023, August 8). *American Airlines participates in first-of-its-kind research on contrail avoidance.* American Airlines. https://news.aa.com/news/news-details/2023/American-Airlines-participates-in-first-of-its-kind-research-on-contrail-avoidance-CORP-OTH-08/default.aspx

Next Move Strategy Consulting. (2023, January). *Artificial intelligence market size and share | analysis - 2030.* NM. https://www.nextmsc.com/report/artificial-intelligence-market

Oladele, A. (2019, March 14). *AI opportunities: Top 9 expectations.* Velvetech. https://www.velvetech.com/blog/ai-opportunities-top-6-expectations/

Palaha, J. (2023, December 5). *5 alarming limitations of artificial intelligence in 2024 and the vital role of human expertise.* Jatinder Palaha. https://www.jatinderpalaha.com/limitations-of-artificial-intelligence/

Payani, A. (2023, March 8). *Council post: Embracing the future: How AI is revolutionizing marketing and sales.* Forbes. https://www.forbes.com/sites/forbesbusinesscouncil/2023/03/08/embracing-the-future-how-ai-is-revolutionizing-marketing-and-sales/?sh=21b93f91bcc2

Pratt, M. K. (2023, June 1). *15 AI risks businesses must confront and how to address them.* EnterpriseAI. https://www.techtarget.com/searchenterpriseai/feature/5-AI-risks-businesses-must-confront-and-how-to-address-them

Quantum Analytics NG. (2023, September 5). *The impact of artificial intelligence on data analytics.* LinkedIn. https://www.linkedin.com/pulse/impact-artificial-intelligence-data-analytics-quantum-analytics-ng

Ramos, C. (2023, February 28). *UCLA synthetic data workshop.* UCLA Mathematics. https://ww3.math.ucla.edu/announcements_ugrad/ucla-synthetic-data-workshop/

Research Report. (2019, May). *Emerging business opportunities in AI.* CompTIA. https://www.comptia.org/content/research/emerging-business-opportunities-in-ai

Rickerby, M. (2020, January 4). *Walmart supply chain: Winning at inventory logistics.* Extensiv. https://www.extensiv.com/blog/supply-chain-management/walmart

Robbins, T. (2020). *Meet Sophia, world's first AI humanoid robot | Tony Robbins* [Video]. YouTube. https://www.youtube.com/watch?v=Sq36J9pNaEo

Robertson, A. (2023, May 24). *I tried the AI novel-writing tool everyone hates, and it's better than I expected.* The Verge. https://www.theverge.com/2023/5/24/23732252/sudowrite-story-engine-ai-generated-cyberpunk-novella

Saballa, J. (2023, March 9). *Boeing, Shield AI collaborate on large ai-piloted aircraft.* The Defense Post. https://www.thedefensepost.com/2023/03/09/boeing-shield-ai-aircraft/

Sahota, N. (2023, February 21). *AI in business: Benefits, challenges & more.* LinkedIn. https://www.linkedin.com/pulse/ai-business-benefits-chal

lenges-more-neil-sahota-%E8%90%A8%E5%86%A0%E5%86%9B-

Shah, S. (2023, July 7). *How Threads became one of the fastest growing apps ever.* Time. https://time.com/6292957/threads-fastest-growing-apps/

Shrivastav, M. (2022). Barriers related to AI implementation in supply chain management. *Journal of Global Information Management (JGIM), 30*(8), 1–19. https://doi.org/10.4018/JGIM.296725

Sinelnikov, D. (2023, September 13). *The future of AI in business: Predictions and how to prepare.* Forbes. https://www.forbes.com/sites/forbesagencycouncil/2023/09/13/the-future-of-ai-in-business-predictions-and-how-to-prepare/?sh=5ca26b1460dd

Stewart, C. (2023, September 28). *AI in healthcare market size worldwide 2030.* Statista. https://www.statista.com/statistics/1334826/ai-in-healthcare-market-size-worldwide/

Team ACV. (2023, October 17). *Consumers are geeking out over these best self-driving cars of 2023.* ACV. https://www.acvauctions.com/blog/best-self-driving-cars

The Team at CallMiner. (2019, June 4). *50 examples of machine learning & AI in data analysis.* CallMiner. https://callminer.com/blog/smart-implementation-machine-learning-ai-data-analysis-50-examples-use-cases-insights-leveraging-ai-ml-data-analytics

This Morning. (2023). *Meet Ameca! The world's most advanced robot* [Video]. YouTube. https://www.youtube.com/watch?v=vE9tIYGyRE8

Thomas, M. (2022, July 6). *16 examples of AI in supply chain and logistics.* Built In. https://builtin.com/artificial-intelligence/ai-in-supply-chain

Thormundsson, B. (2022, March 17). *AI's global impact on job creation and elimination 2022.* Statista. https://www.statista.com/statistics/791992/worldwide-jobs-creation-elimination-due-to-ai/

Thormundsson, B. (2023, October 6). *Artificial intelligence market size 2030.* Statista. https://www.statista.com/statistics/1365145/artificial-intelligence-market-size

"TOP 25 SHARING KNOWLEDGE QUOTES." A-Z Quotes. Accessed January 18, 2024. https://www.azquotes.com/quotes/topics/sharing-knowledge.html

Top 30 tools artificial intelligence (AI) tools list. (2023, December 5). Intellipaat. https://intellipaat.com/blog/top-artificial-intelligence-tools/

Vaccalluzzo, D. (2023, July 16). *Expert systems: History and evolution.* AIBYBYTE.

https://www.aibybyte.ai/artificial-intelligence/history-and-evolution-of-expert-systems/

Van Hoek, R., & Lacity, M. (2023, November 21). *How global companies use AI to prevent supply chain disruptions*. Harvard Business Review. https://hbr.org/2023/11/how-global-companies-use-ai-to-prevent-supply-chain-disruptions

Vettorino, M. Z. (2023, August 24). *Our 13 favorite AI website design tools*. HubSpot. https://blog.hubspot.com/website/ai-website-design-tools

Wall Street Journal. (2021, December 21). *What NASA's Perseverance Rover has learned after 10 months on Mars | WSJ* [Video]. YouTube. https://www.youtube.com/watch?v=WrTHX8t0yl8

Web Admin. (2023, December 18). *Mastering Arduino projects: Harnessing the power of state machines for efficient control*. Innofy. https://innofy.co/dev/embedded/mastering-arduino-projects-harnessing-the-power-of-state-machines-for-efficient-control/

What is an autonomous car? – how self-driving cars work. (2019). Synopsys. https://www.synopsys.com/automotive/what-is-autonomous-car.html

Wilowski, M. (2023, August 9). *Google AI and American Airlines tested ways to reduce climate impact of flights*. Investopedia. https://www.investopedia.com/google-is-helping-airlines-mitigate-their-climate-impact-7574683

Zapanta, T. (2023, February 28). *The impact of AI on business*. MicroSourcing. https://www.microsourcing.com/learn/blog/the-impact-of-ai-on-business/

Zhinko, D. (2018, April 26). *Salesforce AI: What Einstein has for marketing, sales and service*. Science Soft. https://www.scnsoft.com/blog/salesforce-ai-for-marketing-sales-and-service

www.ingramcontent.com/pod-product-compliance
Lightning Source LLC
LaVergne TN
LVHW041212050326
832903LV00021B/583